GROSS
GUIDES
TO PSYCHOLOGY
WJEC AS

RICHARD GROSS

JOHN GRIFFIN

HODDER
EDUCATION
AN HACHETTE UK COMPANY

Picture credits

The authors and publishers would like to thank the following for the use of photographs in this volume:

Figure 2.1 © Vivid Pixels – Fotolia; Figure 3.1 © Brebca – Fotolia; Figure 3.2 © World Illustrated/Photoshot; Figure 4.2 © ClassicStock/TopFoto; Figure 4.3 © Corbis/SuperStock; Figure 6.1 © cphoto – Fotolia; Figure 6.5 © Maroš Markovič – Fotolia; Figures 6.6 and 6.9 from the film Obedience © 1968 by Stanley Milgram; © renewed 1993 by Alexandra Milgram; Figure 7.4 © Poresh – Fotolia; Figure 7.5 © snookless7 – Fotolia.com; Figure 8.5 © HO/Reuters/Corbis; Figure 9.3 © Monkey Business – Fotolia; Figure 9.4 © Chris Fourie – Fotolia; Figure 9.6 © Jan S. – Fotolia; Figure 9.7 © TopFoto; Figure 12.1 © Laurence Gough – Fotolia; Figure of bullseye used throughout © arrow – Fotolia; Figure of open book used throughout © blackred/iStockphoto.

Also:

The tables on page 55 are reprinted from Journal of Verbal Learning and Verbal Behavior, 13, E. Loftus and J. Palmer, 'Reconstruction of automobile destruction: An example of the interaction between language and memory', pp.585–9, 1974, with permission from Elsevier.

Every effort has been made to trace and acknowledge ownership of copyright. The publishers will be glad to make suitable arrangements with any copyright holders whom it has not been possible to contact.

Orders: please contact Bookpoint Ltd, 130 Milton Park, Abingdon, Oxon OX14 4SB. Telephone: (44) 01235 827720. Fax: (44) 01235 400454. Lines are open from 9.00 to 5.00, Monday to Saturday, with a 24-hour message answering service. You can also order through our website www.hoddereducation.co.uk
If you have any comments to make about this, or any of our other titles, please send them to educationenquiries@hodder.co.uk

British Library Cataloguing in Publication Data
A catalogue record for this title is available from the British Library

ISBN: 9781444168105

Published 2012
Impression number   10 9 8 7 6 5 4 3 2 1
Year   2016, 2015, 2014, 2013, 2012

Hachette UK's policy is to use papers that are natural, renewable and recyclable products and made from wood grown in sustainable forests. The logging and manufacturing processes are expected to conform to the environmental regulations of the country of origin.

Illustrations by Barking Dog Art and DC Graphic Design Limited, Swanley Village, Kent
Typeset by DC Graphic Design Limited, Swanley Village, Kent.

Printed in Italy for Hodder Education, An Hachette UK Company, 338 Euston Road, London NW1 3BH by LEGO

Contents

How to use this book

This book will help you revise for your WJEC AS Psychology exams. It is designed so that you can use it alongside any appropriate textbook, including *WJEC Psychology for AS* by Julia Russell and Matt Jarvis (Hodder Education, 2011). You can also use it with Richard Gross's *Psychology: The Science of Mind and Behaviour*, and if you choose to do so we have included page references to appropriate material in this book.

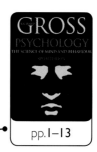

pp.1–13

Each of the ten core studies is covered, with the headline facts and knowledge you will need for each, accompanied by evaluation material to help you reach for those top marks.

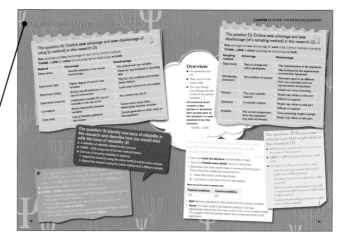

The four approaches and research methods are also covered in a colourful and exciting way, to help you retain and recall the information.

John Griffin is a Senior Examiner and at the end of the book you will find his guidance on preparing for the exams!

Introduction

There are at least three intertwined strands to the biological approach (BIO) to psychology. These are studies of the brain and its actions, the use of evolution as an explanatory device, and the recent development of DNA/genetic studies. They cannot be separated completely today, but behavioural genetics only began in the 1990s, whereas the other two date effectively from the explosion in scientific understanding during the second half of the nineteenth century. The brain is the most complex biological entity known to humans. Until the development of the computer, the main methods of understanding the brain came from dissections, case studies and animal experimentation. None of these methods gave any more than partial glimpses of brain operation. Chemical and physical treatments of brain disorders were often without understanding or explanation – the equivalent of hitting a car engine with a hammer to get it started. Modern scanning methods have revolutionised biological investigation and made direct real-time visual observation possible. Using evolution to explain human behaviour began in the late nineteenth century but has been problematic ever since, as there is no concrete evidence of actual human behaviour in prehistory – fossils do not show behaviour! Consequently, most theories demonstrate as much about our modern attitudes as they do about prehistoric humans.

DNA analysis has begun to answer some questions about the development of humans, but the role of genes in behaviour is still a matter of scientific investigation and dispute (especially human language and genetic adaptation). Exactly how the brain works is the greatest scientific mystery of our time and we seem almost as far off as we were 50 years ago, fMRI notwithstanding.

The question: 1a) Outline two assumptions of the biological approach (4)

Assumption 1: Behaviour can be explained with reference to specific structures in the brain

All behaviour is ultimately produced by the operation of systems that connect specific localised regions of the brain. The cortex is largely responsible for thought, language, vision and movement, whereas fine movement and skill execution are dominated by the action of the cerebellum.

Assumption 2: Aspects of behaviour can be explained by the action of neurotransmitters

These chemicals are agents of communication between neurons at the synapse, stimulating or inhibiting the action of the receptive neuron. Examples include melatonin (influences sleep/wake cycles) and serotonin (sleep, arousal and mood).

▲ **Figure 1.1** Can behaviour be explained with reference to our evolutionary history?

Alternative assumption: Behaviour can be explained with reference to human evolutionary history

Much of our behaviour is determined to some extent by our primate inheritance and the environment that shaped our unique adaptation for survival. Humans are, as a result, intensely social animals, who developed cooperative and planning skills in hostile food-gathering environments.

GROSS
PSYCHOLOGY
THE SCIENCE OF MIND AND BEHAVIOUR
SIXTH EDITION

pp.28–33

The question: 1b) Describe the General Adaptation Syndrome (GAS) (8)

All living organisms have to react to changes in their environment, whether automatically or with a subsequent learnt response. Hans Selye (1947) experimented on rats to see how their body chemistry responded to threats in their environment. He theorised that the basic changes in mammals were the same regardless of the nature of the threat (e.g. extreme temperature, drugs, over-exercise) and that this 'triad' of 'non-specific' responses – the body's defence against stress – was named the General Adaptation Syndrome (GAS).

Alarm reaction

The sympathetic nervous system (SNS) activates the body for action. This is called the 'fight or flight' response. There is temporary diversion of blood to the large muscles of the body, pain detection is suppressed and the body performs an involuntary set of movements called the 'orienting response' (move sensors towards the potential threat, tense the muscles and make evasive moves). The hypothalamus triggers adrenaline and noradrenaline release from the adrenal medulla, which in turn triggers mechanisms to combat the stress for a longer period of time.

Resistance or adaptation

If the threat does not go away, the body moves towards long-term protection. It secretes further hormones, including corticosteroids from the adrenal cortex that increase blood sugar levels to sustain energy and raise blood pressure. Overuse by the body's defence mechanism in this phase eventually leads to disease. If this adaptation phase continues for a prolonged period of time, fatigue will occur, pain will increase and concentration will lapse. This period varies greatly depending on the nature of the threat and the body's already existing reserves.

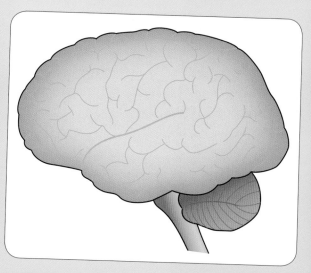

▲ **Figure 1.2** The biological approach is the study of the brain and its actions

Exhaustion

In this stage, the body has run out of its reserve of body energy and immunity. Mental, physical and emotional resources suffer heavily. The body experiences 'adrenal exhaustion'. Blood sugar levels decrease as the adrenals become depleted, leading to decreased stress tolerance, progressive mental and physical exhaustion, illness and collapse. Continually high cortisol levels lead to suppression of the immune system.

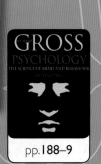

GROSS
PSYCHOLOGY
THE SCIENCE OF MIND AND BEHAVIOUR
SIXTH EDITION

pp. 188–9

The question: 2) Describe how the biological approach has been applied in either psychosurgery or chemotherapy (12)

Psychosurgery

What is the main assumption of the biological approach?	The main assumption of the biological approach is that behaviour can be explained with reference to specific structures and functions of the brain.
How does this assumption link with the general aim of biological therapies?	Biological therapies are based on altering structures or functions of the brain in order to change behaviour in some way, whether physically or chemically.
What is the aim of psychosurgery, and what biological assumptions link with this?	Psychosurgery aims to alter structures in the brain, more specifically the frontal lobes, in order to alter or delete undesirable patterns of behaviour as a consequence.
What is the procedure of psychosurgery?	Psychosurgery has a long history. A process called trepanning or trephining - cutting a hole in the skull to relieve intracranial pressure - has been practised for possibly 40,000 years, and is still an emergency medical procedure used today.
	Modern psychosurgery was born when Moniz noticed a research report that chimps showed less anxiety when the prefrontal cortex was surgically severed. He went on to try this on humans using a wire loop (leucotome) inserted into the frontal lobe by a hole in the skull, and then rotated to remove or sever pieces of lobe.
	Initially influenced by Moniz, Walter Freeman broke with him in the 1940s and popularised a crude and dangerous version of the leucotomy, using an ice-pick inserted or even hammered through the orbit of the eye up into the brain (transorbital lobotomy). He often did this 'on the road', with local anaesthetic and negligent antiseptic procedures!
	Psychosurgery became very popular, especially after the Second World War, with an estimated 40,000 lobotomies in the USA, 17,000 in the UK and many more throughout Europe. These procedures fell into disrepute due to the introduction of major tranquillisers and major political and legal challenges in the USA during the 1960s and 1970s.
	Modern neurosurgery uses MRI scans to locate precise areas to operate on. Areas are burnt away via electrodes or using focused radiation (gamma knife). These operations are successfully used for obsessive-compulsive disorder (OCD), depression, eating disorders and Parkinson's disease.

Chemotherapy

What is the main assumption of the biological approach?	The main assumption of the biological approach is that behaviour can be explained with reference to specific structures and functions of the brain.
How does this assumption link with the general aim of biological therapies?	Biological therapies are based on altering structures or functions of the brain in order to change behaviour in some way, whether physically or chemically.
What is the aim of chemotherapy, and what biological assumptions link with this?	Chemotherapy aims generally to alter the chemistry of the brain, usually in transmission at the synapse. This changes the nature of a behaviour or emotion governed by the action of those neurons.
What is the procedure of chemotherapy?	Psychotropic (mind-changing) drugs are classified according to their target behaviours; the main groupings are of drugs to tackle anxiety-based disorders, depression, and psychotic conditions such as schizophrenia.

Anxiolytics reduce anxiety, and since they tend to calm patients are also known as minor tranquillisers. In larger doses they have sedative effects (i.e. induce sleep) and they are also very addictive.

There are many antidepressants, such as modified tricyclics, which have a variety of blocking effects on various neurotransmitters or the enzymes that break down the transmitters. SSRIs (specific serotonin reuptake inhibitors) are the more common drug of choice today; they make more serotonin available at the synapse by blocking its re-absorption, and therefore lighten moods.

Antipsychotics are also known as major tranquillisers and are used to treat the unusual (or positive) symptoms of major disorders, such as hallucinations, delusions and psychomotor excitement.

Delivery of drugs is either oral or by injection. Oral delivery gives slower absorption and requires a higher dose due to losses during digestion, but is a very flexible method; injection requires a second person, has potential for infection, is invasive, but is more effective for a smaller dosage.

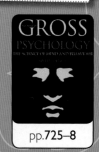

▲ **Figure 1.3** Psychosurgery aims to physically alter the structure of the brain

GROSS
PSYCHOLOGY
THE SCIENCE OF MIND AND BEHAVIOUR

pp.725–8

The question: 3a) Evaluate two strengths of the biological approach (6)

✔ BIO uses the scientific approach and scientific methods, proceeding from observations through experimental tests to application of knowledge. Testing is carried out in a systematic way and repeated to provide reliable results. Modern brain research uses scanning techniques to locate parts of the brain that function during specific tasks. Brain research has identified neurochemicals and their functions. This knowledge is then applied – for example, in brain operations such as capsulotomy, and in chemotherapy with SSRIs.

✔ BIO has provided physical therapies, especially chemotherapy, that have been massively effective in treating the effects of mental disease and psychological disorder. Drug treatment of mental disorder has enabled millions of people to lead relatively normal lives. The use of lithium has helped those with bipolar disorder to have controlled moods; the use of SSRIs such as Prozac has helped people with depression, and tranquillisers have enabled people with schizophrenia to lead more normal lives, though with side effects.

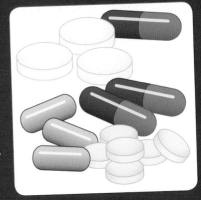

▲ **Figure 1.4** The biological approach has enabled the development of important drug therapies

The question: 3b) Evaluate two weaknesses of the biological approach (6)

✘ BIO ignores everything except biological effects, and especially ignores social causes of behaviour. This is a reductionist approach. As social animals, much of our social behaviour is determined and influenced by other people, so to ignore these effects is to ignore a major cause of behaviour. We can overrule our biology in some cases, for social and moral reasons. For example, instead of mating with any partner, who we mate with is strongly influenced by culture, such as what is currently fashionable

✘ In BIO, individual differences are ignored and generalisations made about all humans in a way that diminishes and ignores the individual (called a 'nomothetic approach'). The person, their personality and what makes them unique is ignored. Individual body chemistry differences can mean totally different responses and behaviours — for example, for the same dosage of a drug. The tranquilliser Valium produces emotional disconnection in most patients, but violent rage for some, when provoked. Unlike males, female hormone cycles alter body chemistry and behaviour. Equally, gender differences do not mean automatic differences in behaviour.

Maximising the marks

Each strength and weakness should be explained using the **Point – Explain – Example (PEE)** structure.

Maximum marks are obtained for:
● detailed and technically correct 'Explain'
● detailed and technically correct 'Example'.

GROSS
PSYCHOLOGY
THE SCIENCE OF MIND AND BEHAVIOUR

pp.52–6

The question: 5) Explain and evaluate the methodology used by the biological approach (12)

METHOD	DESCRIPTION	EXAMPLE	STRENGTHS	WEAKNESSES
Case study	A single person is studied in depth, usually because some brain damage has occurred	Famous examples include Phineas Gage (prefrontal lobes and personality). HM, Clive Wearing (severe amnesia)	◖ Provides a large amount of information ◖ A starting point for all other neurological investigations	◖ Reliability issues – findings have to be repeated ◖ Validity issues as data collection by the researcher(s) may be distorted by their hypotheses
Dissection	Brains of dead people are taken to pieces and structures detected and mapped. Damage to an area can be linked to the person's behaviour in life.	Routine post-mortem (e.g. Broca's study of 'Tan')	◖ Has given most of our information about structures in the brain ◖ Highly reliable and detailed information from millions of post-mortems	◖ Person has to be dead, so cannot respond! ◖ Information about behaviour in life is retrospective and subject to distortion or lack of relevant detail
EEG	Surface sensors on the scalp detect electrical currents caused by chemical changes in the brain. These are recordable as waves of activity.	Used extensively in sleep research (e.g. by Dement) to monitor levels of consciousness	◖ Very useful for monitoring levels and types of consciousness ◖ Detailed information in real time	◖ Can only give general information about brain activity ◖ Does not target specific structures easily
Brain scan PET	The metabolism of radioactive glucose in the brain is detected	Raine's study of brain dysfunction in violent criminals	◖ Shows which brain structures are active during tasks	◖ Costly ◖ Somewhat risky (radiation)
Brain scan MRI	Hydrogen atoms are 'wobbled' by magnetic fields; different densities of tissue wobble differently; detectors provide detailed images	Maguire's study of London taxi drivers' memories pinpointed changes in the hippocampus following extensive route learning ('The Knowledge')	◖ Very detailed and no radiation hazards ◖ Shows where activity is taking place but not what activity specifically	◖ Takes a long time (over 20 minutes) ◖ Participant has to be fully cooperative and lie still!

Introduction

In the late nineteenth century there were several approaches to psychology in existence. Many experimental psychologists were looking at the operation of the sensory systems and memory, and Freud was developing his particular brand of applied psychology (the psychodynamic approach) through his therapeutic work. Many of these psychologists also relied on thinking about their own behaviour as well (introspection).

The behaviourist approach (BEH) grew partly from the wish to model psychology on the physical sciences, partly from a rejection of introspection as too subjective a basis for psychology, and a little bit from Watson's desire for wealth and status. Its historical starting point was Watson's presidential address to the American Psychological Association in 1915, and its two main theoretical pillars were Pavlov's work on the association of stimuli (classical conditioning) and, later, Skinner's work on how changes in the environment operate to change behaviour (operant conditioning).

The question: 1a) Outline two assumptions of the behaviourist approach (4)

Assumption 1: Human behaviour is caused and influenced by events in our environment alone

Behaviourists see humans as born as blank slates, with no predetermined behaviours. Human behaviour is created through the operation of the principal processes of learning – classical conditioning, operant conditioning and social learning.

▲ Figure 2.1 The behaviourist approach sees humans as blank slates, with behaviours being learnt rather than innate

Alternative Assumption 1: Skinner's assumption

Radical behaviourism assumes that the experiences we label as mental events are essentially fictions, and the behaviour attributed to them can be more effectively explained in other ways – that is, without recourse to intentions, thoughts or plans, and making causal links between events in the environment and the behaviour of the organism.

Assumption 2: Psychologists should focus on observable, measurable events in order to be scientific

Since mental events cannot be directly observed or measured, they should not be included in scientific explanations of behaviour. Therefore the behaviourist approach rejects self-reports and opinions.

Alternative assumption

WJEC also accepts descriptions of classical conditioning and operant conditioning as assumptions.

If you wish to use these, follow the PEE method (Point – Explain – Example), making sure there is a technically accurate 'Explain' at the core of your answer.

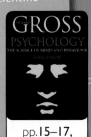

GROSS
PSYCHOLOGY
THE SCIENCE OF MIND AND BEHAVIOUR
6TH EDITION

pp.15–17, 38–9

The question: 1b) Describe the social learning theory of aggression (8)

Theory 1 Social learning theory of aggression

Aggression is a social transaction between two animals, which may or may not involve violence. It is a normal aspect of animal (and human) behaviour and a major form of communication about territory or possession of objects.

Social learning theory (SLT) assumes that the environment will strongly influence behaviour, and that learning by observation will take place. Humans are predisposed to **imitate** (copy) or **model** (do generally similar behaviour). This behaviour is then **reinforced** by consequences (operant conditioning). Therefore humans will observe others using aggression successfully, and then imitate that aggression in similar circumstances. If they are also successful (rewarded), the behaviour is **reinforced** and will continue, often being tried in different situations (**generalised**).

Theory 2

Bandura set out to demonstrate the SLT theory of aggression by taking 72 children aged between 3 and 6 years from the Chicago University nursery. Having first rated their natural aggression by observing them in normal play, he exposed them individually for 10 minutes to an **adult model** in a playroom. The adult model either played quietly or behaved aggressively towards a large, polythene, inflatable, self-righting doll (known as a 'Bobo doll' in the USA). Both male and female models were used, and they were scripted to use physical and verbal abuse in the aggression conditions.

The children were then taken to a second room where they were not allowed to play with attractive toys – this was to upset and **arouse** them. It was thought that arousal would make the children more likely to react aggressively.

The final room had attractive toys and a 'Bobo' doll. The children's **behaviour** in that room was observed and recorded for 20 minutes, sampling behaviour every 5 seconds.

Bandura found that children largely **copied** the behaviour of the model, aggressive or non-aggressive. They were more likely to copy the **same-sex model** and boys were slightly more likely to be aggressive than girls. Many of them found the aggression of the female model to be slightly disturbing.

▲ **Figure 2.2** A bobo doll

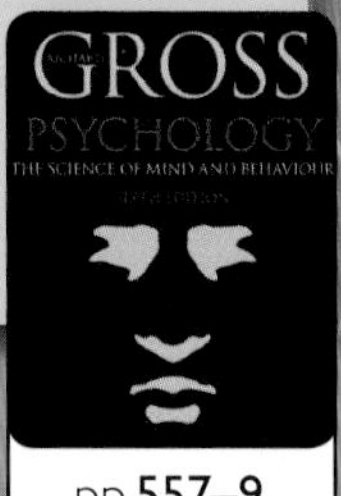

GROSS
PSYCHOLOGY
THE SCIENCE OF MIND AND BEHAVIOUR

pp.557–9,
455–62

The question: 2) Describe how the behaviourist approach has been applied in either systematic desensitisation or aversion therapy (12)

Systematic desensitisation

What is the main assumption of the behaviourist approach?	The main assumption of the behaviourist approach is that all behaviour is learnt in response to changes in the environment.
How does this assumption link with the general aim of behavioural therapies?	Behavioural therapies all assume that a maladaptive (problem) behaviour can be altered or extinguished by a suitable training programme based on learning principles.
What is the aim of systematic desensitisation, and what behavioural assumptions link with this?	The therapy involves classical conditioning a new response (relaxation) to a stimulus that previously evoked an unjustifiable fear response (phobia), such as extreme anxiety over the presence of birds. This is called response substitution. Behaviourists believe that all responses can be relearnt or modified using conditioning techniques.
What is the procedure of systematic desensitisation?	There are three steps to the process of systematic desensitisation of a phobia:

1. The patient learns a relaxation response in a series of training exercises led by the therapist. Some patients learn very quickly, others take a long time.
2. While this is continuing, the patient constructs a graduated scale of phobic response, from low anxiety (e.g. a picture of a bird) to extreme anxiety (e.g. a bird perched on the hand). This is then used as a ladder of progress in therapy.
3. The patient is then exposed to the lowest step on the ladder and practises the relaxation response. Once they can relax consistently, they are exposed to the next level of anxiety.

Success is judged either by relaxation achieved at the most extreme step of the ladder, or when the patient judges their life to be acceptably improved.

▲ **Figure 2.3** Systematic desensitisation can be used to treat phobias

Aversion therapy

What is the main assumption of the behaviourist approach?	The main assumption of the behaviourist approach is that all behaviour is learnt in response to changes in the environment.
How does this assumption link with the general aim of behavioural therapies?	Behavioural therapies all assume that a maladaptive (problem) behaviour can be altered or extinguished by a suitable training programme based on learning principles.
What is the aim of aversion therapy, and what behavioural assumptions link with this?	The therapy involves removing an undesirable response to a stimulus (e.g. pleasure and alcohol) by associating one stimulus with another (e.g. alcohol and severe nausea) using classical conditioning.
What is the procedure of aversion therapy?	In the case of alcohol, patients are given a saline solution with an emetic (drug to cause nausea and vomiting). They are then given a glass of whisky, which they smell, taste and then drink. If vomiting does not occur, they then get further whisky and beer plus the emetic. Further repeats involve a wider range of alcoholic drinks. In between treatments, soft drinks are

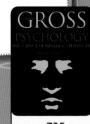

▲ **Figure 2.4** Aversion therapy, a behavioural treatment, can be used to treat alcoholism

provided so that aversion does not develop to all drinks and to promote the use of alcohol substitutes.

A controversial use has been to treat sexual orientation and preferences by pairing erotic pictures with electric shocks; however, this has been largely disused since the 1970s, following changes in social attitudes.

GROSS
PSYCHOLOGY

p.735

11

The question: 3a) Evaluate two strengths of the behaviourist approach (6)

✔ BEH highlights the way the behaviour of others causes and reinforces our behaviour. We learn via **observation** (e.g. social learning of aggression) and other people **reinforce** our behaviour, such as parents approving or disapproving of things we do (operant conditioning). We also learn **associations** between objects and internal states, such as between food consumption and pleasure (classical conditioning).

✔ BEH emphasises the scientific nature of psychology by shifting the focus onto observable and measurable events.

✔ Ideas and thoughts are only reportable, not directly measurable, so may not be true, accurate or reliable. To gain accurate knowledge, only measurable events can be used in psychology if it is to be scientific in the same way as physics.

The question: 3b) Evaluate two weaknesses of the behaviourist approach (6)

✗ BEH does not accept mental events as causes, although they clearly can be. We can decide to do something we have never done before (e.g. take a chance on a new experience), and people can resist reinforcements and punishments purely for an idea they may have (e.g. resisting torture for a cause they believe in). A complete psychology has to account for some forms of mental events to be credible.

✗ BEH can offer no explanation at all of many important human behaviours, such as creativity and humour. Creativity involves producing something that has not been done before in the same way and is recognised by others as unique and worthwhile in some way. Examples are found in art and music. Behaviourism may be able to point to the acquisition of influences and skills (e.g. keyboard technique), but cannot show how these activities develop in total, because most of the unique activities are thought processes, and thus unobservable.

▲ Figure 2.5 The behaviourist approach can offer no explanation for creativity

Maximising the marks

Each strength and weakness should be explained using the **Point – Explain – Example (PEE)** structure.

Maximum marks are obtained for:

● detailed and technically correct 'Explain'

● detailed and technically correct 'Example'.

The question: 5) Explain and evaluate the methodology used by the behaviourist approach (12)

Method	Description	Example	Strengths	Weaknesses
Animal experiments	Standard investigation of cause-effect relationships using highly controlled, laboratory-based studies	Pavlov's use of dogs to investigate digestion, leading to the investigation of conditioning	Animals: ◊ are cheap ◊ have faster reproductive cycles ◊ do not have to consent ◊ can be harmed more than humans	◊ Ethical concerns have led to a huge reduction in animal experiments ◊ Animals are not direct analogues for humans in many behaviours (e.g. thoughts, sex) ◊ Animal behaviour in unnatural circumstances is abnormal
Human 'field' experiments	Highly controlled studies in natural settings, usually some form of institution where considerable behavioural control is normal	Token economy studies in mental hospitals; Bandura's study of aggression in children	◊ Actual human participants ◊ Partly realistic situations (ecological validity) ◊ High levels of control ensure valid conclusions about cause-effect relationships can be made	◊ Ethical problem of consent from patients or children ◊ Ethical problem of freedom to leave the study ◊ Ethical problem of fair treatment - many token economy studies used rewards that should be part of normal life (e.g. cinema visits)
Case studies	In-depth study of a single individual, often typical of behavioural therapies	Wolpe's development of systematic desensitisation via study of animals and then treatment of anxiety disorders	◊ High levels of qualitative information ◊ Usually conducted very ethically ◊ Can inform further research ◊ Generally ecologically valid	◊ Cannot achieve high levels of control ◊ Much information is subjective self-report from participants

Introduction

The psychodynamic approach (PSY) is indelibly associated with the work of one of the flawed geniuses of the early twentieth century, **Sigmund Freud**. Freud was not totally original, but more than anyone he altered forever the way we would look at the world. Psychological problems were once the realm of priests and shamans, but Freud located the devils and demons not only within the person's brain, but formed by childhood experiences and largely hidden from conscious view.

Freud was originally a neurologist (in modern terms) who became convinced of the power of the mind to imitate and influence physical disorder. He utilised hypnotism initially, but then moved on to his signature techniques of free association and dream analysis. He struggled for some years as a private practitioner before his elevation as one of the icons of the early twentieth century.

The idea that our behaviour is often determined by unconscious forces, and that dreams could reveal the origins of these forces, became highly fashionable to the middle classes of Europe and the USA; these ideas also pervaded literature and art forms, including cinema. Britain became Freud's final home in the late 1930s, and one of his daughters, Anna, was a leading influence on the development of British therapeutic psychology, although explicit Freudian analysis soon gave way to a more pragmatic British approach.

Freudian psychology became increasingly marginal from the 1960s onwards, under attack from experimental psychologists and therapists alike. Freud's insights into human behaviour have received some rehabilitation, and modern research methods, including fMRI, have been used to re-examine Freudian hypotheses, demonstrating that some may not be as outlandish as previously thought.

The question: 1a) Outline two assumptions of the psychodynamic approach (4)

Assumption 1: Importance of early experience

Adult personality and behaviour have roots in childhood experiences. The biggest influence in childhood is the parents and the parenting a child receives. The relationships with parents are the template for future ways of dealing with other people, and the levels of love and security offered to the child deeply influence their personal stability and mental health.

Assumption 2: Influence of the unconscious mind

The unconscious is a major determinant of the way we respond to events in our lives. We do not have access to the memories contained in the unconscious, many of them being of powerful and disturbing events in our childhoods that directly affect the way we see the world and react to it. The unconscious is only visible during dreams or uncovered in therapy.

▲ **Figure 3.1** The role of early childhood experiences is very important in the psychodynamic approach

The question: 1b) Describe Freud's theory of personality development (8)

A major influence on personality is the dominance of a part of the core personality as conceived by Freud. A **dominant id** means a lack of moral control over behaviour (a typical criminal profile) with too much self-regard (narcissism). A **dominant superego** leaves someone emotionally frozen and very judgemental, often a profile of religious hardliners. A **dominant ego** can lead to someone being over-rational and too logical in relationships.

Protecting the sense of self (ego) by **defence mechanisms** such as denial is normal, but can lead to over-aggressive behaviour, blaming others or even becoming distanced from real-world events.

One influence on personality formation is when a person gets stuck (**fixated**) in one of the **psychosexual stages**.

An **oral fixation** combined with a **punishing parental style** leads to the formation of an aggressive character with negative thought patterns and paranoia, but if the parental style is **indulgent**, the character formed is dependent, easily fooled and over-indulgent in consumption of food, drink and material things (e.g. a persistent shopper).

If fixation occurs in the potty-training or **anal stage**, and the parents are **punishing**, the personality is called **anal-retentive**. Such a person will be obsessive, obstinate, fussy and miserly. If, however, the parents are **indulgent**, then an **anal-expulsive** character forms. This is the classic binge character, generous, disorganised, prone to losing control of drinking, eating, spending and so on, and often requiring others to take responsibility when they are on a binge.

▲ **Figure 3.2** Sigmund Freud

The question: 2) Describe how the psychodynamic approach has been applied in either free association or dream analysis (12)

Free association

What is the main assumption of the psychodynamic approach?	The unconscious is a major determinant of the way we respond to events in our lives. We do not have access to the memories contained in the unconscious, many of them being of powerful and disturbing events in our childhoods that directly affect the way we see the world and react to it.
How does this assumption link with the central aim of psychodynamic therapies?	Psychodynamic therapies aim to uncover memories buried in the unconscious and bring them into the conscious.
What is the aim of free association, and what psychodynamic assumptions link with this?	By 'allowing the patient to share the contents of their minds, no matter how silly, irrelevant or embarrassing', the therapist may pinpoint where material from the unconscious is blocking recall. The assumption is that psychological defence mechanisms are in operation, preventing the release of the material (Gross 2010).
What is the procedure of free association?	The patient relaxes in a room free of distractions, usually seated, while the therapist sits out of direct view to take notes. Silence is only broken when the pressure of the patient's thoughts leads them to talk; the therapist does not intervene except to confirm 'facts' offered by the patient.
	The therapist makes special notes of topics where there is unusual emotional activity (e.g. the patient seems suddenly upset) or where the flow of talk suddenly stops. It is presumed that the patient has arrived at a place where the flow of thoughts encounters something hidden in the unconscious.
	Once the patient has offered enough of this type of material, the therapist may move to summarising and interpreting the material collected. This is done in a dialogue with the patient, often negotiating meanings of recalled or blocked material. These discussions should lead to breakthroughs where the patient identifies the blocked material and has insight into how this affects their behaviour and personality.
	This insight should lead to the patient being able to take more control of their life.
	Evidence from a number of before-and-after studies (Fonagy 2000) suggests that psychoanalysis is consistently helpful to patients with milder anxiety disorders (neuroses), but less consistent when dealing with severe disorders (psychoses).

Dream analysis

What is the main assumption of the psychodynamic approach?	The unconscious is a major determinant of the way we respond to events in our lives. We do not have access to the memories contained in the unconscious, many of them being of powerful and disturbing events in our childhoods that directly affect the way we see the world and react to it.
How does this assumption link with the general aim of psychodynamic therapies?	Psychodynamic therapies aim to uncover memories buried in the unconscious and bring them into the conscious.
What is the aim of dream analysis, and what psychodynamic assumptions link with this?	Dreams are the 'Royal Road to the unconscious', where desires and memories are released into the realm of the conscious. Dream analysis aims to decode those dreams and relate them to the patient's current problems, assuming that the problem arises from a memory hidden from view by a psychological defence mechanism such as repression. The surface recall of a dream is known as manifest content, and the decoded dream as the latent content - that is, the hidden meaning.
What is the procedure of dream analysis?	The patient relaxes in a room that is free of distractions, usually seated, while the therapist sits out of direct view to take notes. The patient is then asked to report a dream recall in the period since the last therapeutic session.

The therapist makes notes, and either prompts the recall with neutral statements (e.g. 'Go on.'; 'What do you recall next?'), or waits in silence for the patient to start again. The therapist may also note the patient's emotional states during recall and any moments when they seem to falter and halt – especially the material just preceding the halt.

Once the dream content is recorded, it is considered as the manifest content. The goal of the therapist is now to decode the dream to reveal their interpretation of the latent content.

The patient reviews the interpretation and they enter into a dialogue with the therapist to further explore the meaning and implications of the dream. It is expected that the patient will gain insight into their life and problems via this process, repeated again and again.

The goal of the therapy is to increase insight and therefore the patient's control over their own life.

Evidence from a number of before-and-after studies (Fonagy 2000) suggests that psychoanalysis is consistently helpful to patients with milder anxiety disorders (neuroses), but less consistent when dealing with severe disorders (psychoses).

▲ **Figure 3.3**

The question: 3a) Evaluate two strengths of the psychodynamic approach (6)

✔ Has an important focus on the **role of early childhood experience** in affecting the development of personality and future behaviour. The nature of these experiences, and when they occur, has major effects on personality (e.g. fixation in a stage leading to specific character traits). Understanding individual psychology has to take account of early experiences, regardless of whether explicitly Freudian or not.

✔ Draws attention to the **existence of unconscious desires and memories** that can **affect behaviour**, often in a negative or maladaptive way. The desires and memories have been forced into the unconscious by psychological defence mechanisms, such as repression and sublimation. This has been clearly shown in case studies over the last 100 years and eventually by experimentation (e.g. Adams (1996), showed that homophobes were actually more sexually aroused by erotic gay videos than unprejudiced men, which was predicted by Freud as an example of repressed desires).

The question: 3b) Evaluate two weaknesses of the psychodynamic approach (6)

✗ Generally unscientific method of theorising, using case study and interpretation rather than experimentation. Many of the theories are couched in very grandiose or obscure language, speculative or plain wrong. Popper famously used Freud's mechanism of reaction formation to illustrate his criticism of its unscientific nature. Famously, some behaviours can be interpreted in opposite ways depending on the specific bit of Freud's work chosen (e.g. if you deny something has ever happened, you could be using the defence mechanism of denial).

✗ Freudian theory is both **ethnocentric** (largely relevant only to Western European culture) and **androcentric** (focuses largely on males, with weaker theories for females). This is partly a reflection of the paternalistic European society that psychodynamic theory was founded in, where women were seen as a 'weaker sex', and ideas about neurotic behaviour were almost entirely biased to portray women as weak, ineffectual creatures of lower intelligence. Freud himself was aware of these weaknesses in his theories, especially the unsatisfactory and incomplete nature of his theory of the 'Electra complex'.

Maximising the marks

Each strength and weakness should be explained using the **Point – Explain – Example (PEE)** structure.

Maximum marks are obtained for:

● detailed and technically correct 'Explain'

● detailed and technically correct 'Example'.

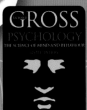

GROSS
PSYCHOLOGY
THE SCIENCE OF MIND AND BEHAVIOUR

pp.674–7

The question: 5) Explain and evaluate the methodology used by the psychodynamic approach (12)

METHOD	DESCRIPTION	EXAMPLE	STRENGTHS	WEAKNESSES
Case study	An individual patient is studied over a period of time, and considerable qualitative material is collected relating to their experience of the world, as well as the therapist's interpretations.	Anna O The Wolfman Little Hans	⟲ Very high-quality information is gained ⟲ Study follows through a single patient, which can reveal stages of progress	⟲ Results usually not representative or generalisable ⟲ Data can be distorted by the therapist's ideology (e.g. selective or biased reporting) ⟲ Can take a long time
Clinical interview	Any interview procedure in a therapeutic setting, but in the Freudian sense, it is one led by the patient's material rather than set questions.	Free association Dream analysis	⟲ Driven by the patient's material	⟲ Material (data) offered by patient may be distorted by transference/counter-transference
Brief focal therapy	A high level of therapeutic activity, in a short period of time, focuses on a very limited area of the patient's problems. (Hoyt 2003)		⟲ Can be practised by clinical psychologists without full analysis training (which takes several years) ⟲ Has been evaluated scientifically as being effective (Fonagy 2000)	⟲ Highly directive, where the therapist pushes the direction of therapy rather than the patient ⟲ Does not tackle the root causes of problems
Interpersonal psychodynamic therapy (IPT)	The therapist becomes a partner and suggests behavioural changes as well as listening and interpreting. The focus is more on the client's current life than on the causes of their problems.		⟲ Has been assessed by several major programmes as being effective for unipolar depression (Elkin 1989; Davison 2004) ⟲ Patient is an active partner in their treatment	

Introduction

The cognitive approach has effectively existed from the time of the first laboratories of psychology in the late nineteenth century. The main areas of interest were memory and the sensory processes. Introspection was also used extensively, particularly as some processes were unmeasurable, such as consciousness.

The approach fell out of fashion in the USA with the advent of behaviourism, somewhat less so in the UK and hardly at all in Europe, where cognition and cognitive development remained central issues for research, with Piaget probably the greatest figure of the twentieth century.

However, as most English textbooks and journals were published in the USA, this neglect was dominant until the behaviourist bubble burst in the late 1950s, partly due to the rise of information theory and the development of the computer. A meeting at the Massachusetts Institute of Technology (MIT) in the USA involved Chomsky's theory of language, Miller's paper on memory and developments leading towards the idea of machine intelligence. This is seen as a marker for the beginning of the 'cognitive revolution'.

In the UK the cognitive flag was kept flying by figures such as Bartlett, Broadbent and Gregory, and cognitive psychology was integral to developments such as robotics, computer programming and machine design (ergonomics). Cognitive psychology also had an impact in development of effective therapies for psychological disorders and spawned many 'New Age' offshoots, such as neurolinguistic programming (NLP).

Cognitive psychology is now part of the multidisciplinary approach to the human brain and its functions known as cognitive neuroscience.

The question: 1a) Outline two assumptions of the cognitive approach (4)

Assumption 1: There is a primary focus on mental processes and their effect on behaviour

The primary source of human behaviour is considered to be the processes and functions of the brain. The cognitive approach itself does not require an understanding of the biology of the brain and how it works, though it does complement the biological approach, which emphasises these things. There is a central role in research in the cognitive approach for the study of human awareness of some of these processes; this is labelled 'consciousness'.

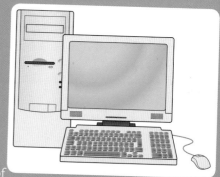

▲ **Figure 4.1** Cognitive psychologists create computer-style models of brain mechanisms

Assumption 2: Current cognitive psychology uses a computer analogy (i.e. all our brains are described as if they were computers)

Since the brain does not reveal its functions by looking at its structure, cognitive psychologists create computer-style models of mechanisms assumed to exist in the brain and then test these models against research findings, modifying, elaborating or discarding the models as appropriate.

GROSS
PSYCHOLOGY
THE SCIENCE OF MIND AND BEHAVIOUR

pp.39–40

The question: 1b) Describe attribution theory (8)

We have a drive to explain events (attribute) that all humans display; this drive applies to both physical and social events. The underlying mechanism is probably a development of a 'threat evaluation' that evolved on top of the automatic GAS responses. It makes survival sense to treat puzzling objects as being alive, and working out what they seem to be doing. This is a **schema** or system that develops through social learning.

There is a possibly **innate bias** towards using '**agency**' explanations (where all objects have intentions), which is thought to lead to religious ideas in some people. This bias is also evident in the **fundamental attribution error** (FAE), where we tend to attribute events to human intentions rather than to the situations they are in. Heider (1958) challenged psychologists to uncover the ways that ordinary people used to understand their world.

Several psychologists created cognitive models; one of the most enduring is **Kelley's Covariation Model** (1967), which uses three dimensions: **consensus, distinctiveness** and **consistency**:

- Consensus: Do other people behave that way in the same situation (high consensus) or not (low consensus)?

- Distinctiveness: Does the target person behave the same way in other situations (low) or is this unusual (high)?

- Consistency: Is this behaviour stable over time – do they always do this (high) or does their behaviour vary (low)?

Kelley suggested that a combination of low consensus, low distinctiveness and high consistency in a person's behaviour led people to make a **personal intention** attribution (also known as **dispositional**); any other combination led to a **situational** attribution (it is the situation they are in).

▲ **Figure 4.2** The development of the computer gave psychologists a new way of thinking about the mind

Alongside the FAE, many people make '**just world**', attributions where people get what they deserve; bad people get their just punishment further along in life. The other main bias is the **actor/observer effect**, where we view our own behaviour as a product of the situation, but other people's as due to their personality or intentions.

GROSS
PSYCHOLOGY
THE SCIENCE OF MIND AND BEHAVIOUR

pp.22–4

The question: 2) Describe how the cognitive approach has been applied in either cognitive behavioural therapy (CBT) or rational emotive therapy (RET) (12)

Cognitive behavioural therapy

What is the main assumption of the cognitive approach?	There is a primary focus on mental processes that direct and govern behaviour: changing these cognitions changes our behaviour.
How does this assumption link with the general aim of cognitive therapies?	Behaviour is directed by schemas, the constantly developing mental structures that individually govern acts of behaviour. Altering these schemas by illuminating or training thought processes will modify behaviour and give the patient more control over their life.
What is the aim of cognitive behavioural therapy (CBT), and what cognitive assumptions link with this?	CBT aims to illuminate and then challenge habitual thought processes (automatic thoughts) that patients have which direct their behaviour. The therapy aims to retrain thought processes so that the patient's behaviour is more functional.
What is the procedure of cognitive behavioural therapy?	A cognitive behavioural therapist would test assumptions by enabling the patient to collect evidence from family, friends and objective sources to support their assumptions. By showing the patient that evidence does not support them, the therapist exposes the irrationality of the patient's assumptions and will also provide a new model of thought for the patient to change their previous behaviour pattern (i.e. 'I am a competent person, therefore I should not have any problem coping with new situations'). Additional behavioural techniques such as operant conditioning (the use of positive and/or negative reinforcements to encourage desired behaviour) and systematic desensitisation (gradual exposure to anxiety-producing situations in order to extinguish the fear response) may then be used to gradually normalise the patient's behaviour.

Rational emotive therapy

What is the main assumption of the cognitive approach?	There is a primary focus on mental processes that direct and govern behaviour; changing these cognitions changes our behaviour.
How does this assumption link with the general aim of cognitive therapies?	Behaviour is directed by schemas, the constantly developing mental structures that individually govern acts of behaviour. Altering these schemas by directing or training thought processes will modify behaviour and give the patient more control over their life.
What is the aim of rational emotive therapy (RET), and what cognitive assumptions link with this?	RET aims to illuminate and then challenge habitual beliefs that patients have which direct their behaviour. Ellis (1957) called these beliefs 'mustabatory' - they must be true in order for the patient to be happy (e.g. everyone must like me for me to be happy). The therapy aims to retrain thought processes so that the patient's behaviour is more functional.
What is the procedure of rational emotive therapy?	Ellis used the ABC model to classify beliefs: A = (activating event) Your girl/boyfriend dumps you! B = (belief) You will never be attractive enough to keep a relationship. C = (consequence) You give up trying to date anyone. Ellis introduced two subsequent stages that occurred in therapy. D = disputing beliefs E = effect of disputing beliefs. There were various ways a therapist would dispute beliefs: ⊃ Disputing logically (does not make sense) ⊃ Disputing empirically (there is no proof of this) ⊃ Disputing pragmatically (having this belief is messing my life up). The effect of disputing moved the patient towards more rational thinking about events, instead of constantly thinking the worst (catastrophising). Ellis emphasised that the therapist had to behave emotionally like a good parent in that they had to have unconditional positive regard (i.e. be warmly tolerant of the patient).

The question: 3a) Evaluate two strengths of the cognitive approach (6)

✔ This approach focuses on the internal mechanisms that govern human experience of the world and the way that these processes direct our behaviour. Models of these processes are linked to observations provided by brain scanning, to try to map the parts of the brain involved. This has been the **most successful** interdisciplinary branch of psychology in the last twenty years and is a major area of psychological research currently.

✔ The approach has provided us with several **non-invasive therapies** (e.g. CBT). These have proved very effective in dealing with psychological problems, especially when linked with behavioural elements (e.g. modelling from SLT). Even schizophrenia has been treated successfully when drug therapy stabilises the patient enough so that rational conversation and planning is possible.

The question: 3b) Evaluate two weaknesses of the cognitive approach (6)

✗ This approach has little to say about the **content** or **quality** of human experience. While there is a role for personal experience and self-report in cognitive therapies, in the main thrust of research there is an almost exclusive focus on brain processes and functions. Therefore it may be deemed both **mechanistic** and **reductionist**, as it does not provide a full psychological account of human behaviour.

✗ Despite the success achieved by using it to drive research, the computer analogy is thoroughly misleading. It is clear to modern science that the **brain is nothing like any current type of computer**, either in structure or processes. Brains are complex biological structures that actively organise and interpret inputs from the environment and also generate unique new outputs (e.g. creative art).

Maximising the marks

Each strength and weakness should be explained using the **Point – Explain – Example (PEE)** structure.

Maximum marks are obtained for:

● detailed and technically correct 'Explain'.

● detailed and technically correct 'Example'.

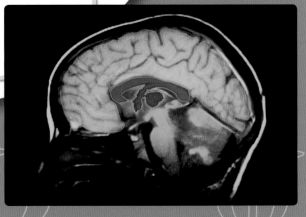

▲ **Figure 4.3** Brain scan

The question: 5) Explain and evaluate the methodology used by the cognitive approach (12)

METHOD	DESCRIPTION	EXAMPLE	STRENGTHS	WEAKNESSES
Case study	A single person is studied in depth, usually because some brain damage has occurred. This allows hypotheses to be developed that are tested experimentally or by seeking other case studies.	Famous examples include HM and Clive Wearing (severe amnesia)	○ Provides a large amount of information ○ A starting point for all other cognitive neuroscience investigations	○ Reliability issues - findings have to be repeated ○ Validity issues as data collection by the researcher(s) may be distorted by their hypotheses
Experiment	Testing is carried out on individuals or small samples.	Loftus & Palmer (1974) on eyewitness testimony	○ Main method for validly establishing cause-effect relationships ○ Highly controlled	○ Often not very much like real life (low ecological validity) ○ Open to biases on the part of both the experimenter and the participant
EEG	Surface sensors on the scalp detect electrical currents caused by chemical changes in the brain. These are recordable as waves of activity.	Used extensively in sleep research (e.g. by Dement) to monitor levels of consciousness	○ Very useful for monitoring levels and types of consciousness ○ Detailed information in real time	○ Can only give general information about brain activity ○ Does not target specific structures easily
Brain scans (PET)	These detect the metabolism of radioactive glucose in the brain.	Raine's study of brain dysfunction in violent criminals	○ Shows which brain structures are active during tasks	○ Costly ○ Somewhat risky (radiation)
Brain scans (MRI)	Hydrogen atoms are 'wobbled' by magnetic fields; different densities of tissue wobble differently; detectors provide detailed images.	Maguire's study of London taxi drivers' memories pinpointed changes in the hippocampus following extensive route learning ('the Knowledge')	○ Very detailed and no radiation hazards ○ Shows where activity is taking place, but not what activity specifically	○ Takes a long time (over 20 minutes) ○ Participant has to be fully cooperative and lie still! ○ Very costly

How to write your answer

Compare: looking for similarities

Uses comparison words:

- both
- each
- equally
- like.
- similarly

Contrast: looking for differences

Uses contrast words:

- but
- in contrast to
- however
- unlike
- quite the opposite to
- instead.

Scientific method used?	Does the approach use a standard set of scientific methods?
Reductionism	Is there one main theme in explanation of behaviour? Are there other plausible factors that influence behaviour? Is the approach too limited in its explanation of behaviour?
Determinism	Is there a possibility of **free will**? How much is behaviour determined? How is behaviour determined?
Usefulness	What has the approach given to humanity? How has it been used in the real world? Are there valid therapies within this approach? What negatives has it produced?
Genetic versus environment	Is there a genetic dimension to this approach? Is there a strong bias to either genetic or environmental explanations? Does modern science back up the approach?
History and current status	How has the approach developed historically? What is the current status of this approach?
View of human nature	Are people viewed as machines – is the approach **mechanistic**? Are people seen as animals or are special qualities explained (e.g. language)? Does the approach explain art, creativity, human emotions, interpersonal behaviours and emotions (e.g. humour, love)?

The mnemonic checklist

Devise a checklist for yourself that is memorable. For example: DRUGS are history, naturally. (Determinism, Reductionism, Usefulness, Genetic, Scientific, History, view of human Nature).

There are **six** possible combinations of approaches for Question 4.

- biological and behavioural
- biological and cognitive
- biological and psychodynamic
- behavioural and cognitive
- behavioural and psychodynamic
- cognitive and psychodynamic.

You may wish to make grids for each.

The question: 4) Compare and contrast the biological and psychodynamic approaches in terms of similarities and differences (12)

Grid for notes

	Biological	Behavioural	Similar or different?
Scientific use?	**Yes** – experiments, observations, case studies, animal behaviour studies, dissection, twin studies, scanning techniques etc.	**Yes** – experiments, observations, animal behaviour studies. Brought scientific rigour to psychology in the early twentieth century.	**Similar**
Reductionism	**Very reductionist.** All behaviour is reduced to the product of brain structures and functions.	**Very reductionist.** All behaviour is seen as produced by the environment alone. Mechanisms include classical and operant conditioning and social learning.	**Similar** but different emphasis
Determinism	**Very deterministic.** Behaviour produced by brain. Role of free will or consciousness not sorted out yet.	**Very deterministic.** Behaviour produced by reinforcements, not free will.	**Similar** but some differences in detail
Usefulness	**Very useful.** Has provided us with most information about human behaviour and functions. Chemotherapy is the most used method to alter and improve behaviour and feelings. However, many of these therapies are invasive and chemotherapy only tackles symptoms, not causes.	**Very useful.** Successful therapies, which are totally non-invasive. However, behavioural techniques can also be used to manipulate and oppress people.	**Similar** in usefulness but some differences in how they are useful
Genetic versus environment	**Genetics is a central part** of this approach, whether immediate inheritance or the effects of evolution.	**Totally ignores genetics** and focuses only on the environment as a determinant of behaviour.	**Different** and diametrically opposite
History and current status	Long history going back centuries and a central part of **neuroscience** today.	Largely important in the early twentieth century, but now **mostly history**.	**Different**
View of human nature	Essentially another animal, though a complex one.	Governed by the same laws as other animals.	**Similar** but different in detail

An example of an opening paragraph

Both approaches use scientific methods in their investigations. Laboratory studies are common to both, as are animal behaviour studies. However, the range of methods is wider in the biological approach as it also uses case studies, dissection, twin studies and various scanning techniques.

Context

Solomon Asch was a Polish immigrant who had a very distinguished career as a social psychologist in the USA.

Work on conformity first came to prominence with Jenness (1932) exploring group estimates of the number of beans in a jar. Participants tended to conform in their judgements after discussing their individual estimates.

Sherif (1936) conducted an experiment on informational conformity. This is where a situation is ambiguous – that is, it could be interpreted in more than one way. We tend to look for clues to enable us to make a decision.

Sherif used the **autokinetic effect**: a stationary light in a dark room will appear to move, because the eye is constantly moving some 20–50 times a second (saccadic movements). He asked participants to judge how far such a light had moved, both individually and with knowledge of other people's results. The range of answers became much narrower in the latter case, with participants tending to conform to the group average. Asch was interested in the fact that many people do not conform even under the strongest social pressure, an interest born from the history of resistance movements in the Second World War.

Asch decided to work with an **unambiguous stimulus**, one that is very clear to the participant. He aimed to look at **normative conformity**, which is whether participants would change their answer towards a group norm, even if their judgement told them otherwise. This is clearly a much more powerful type of conformity, requiring denial of a personal judgement and acceptance of a group norm that is clearly incorrect.

He did not expect any great degree of conformity, rather that most participants would refuse to conform.

▲ Figure 6.1 Jenness's jelly bean experiment

Aim

Asch aimed to test the strength of normative conformity by presenting participants with a group norm regarding a physical judgement that is clearly wrong.

GROSS
PSYCHOLOGY
THE SCIENCE OF MIND AND BEHAVIOUR

pp.401–2

Critical assessment

Perrin and Spencer (1980) suggested that the Asch effect was a 'child of its time'. They carried out an exact replication of the original Asch experiment using engineering, mathematics and chemistry students as subjects. The results were clear-cut: on only one out of 396 trials did an observer join the erroneous majority. They argue that a cultural change has taken place in the value placed on conformity and obedience and in the position of students. In America in the 1950s students were unobtrusive members of society, whereas now they occupy a free, questioning role. This implies that Asch's results were not generalisable cross-culturally.

Nicholson et al. (1985) were more positive, finding that the number of error responses obtained was significantly lower than those reported by Asch, but it was also significantly greater than zero (12 out of the UK sample of 38 and 8 of the US sample of 21 conformed at least once). British and American students did not differ in their responses to unanimous peer-group opinion. This provides some support for Asch.

Lalancette & Standing (1990) repeated the classic experiment and variations, yet no conformity was observed. They concluded that the Asch effect appears to be an unpredictable phenomenon rather than a stable tendency of human behaviour.

Neto (1995) repeated the classic conformity experiment, using women psychology students in a Portuguese university as minority of one unanimous majority group, and control participants. The original procedure was re-enacted as similarly as possible using a computer program. Among participants in the experimental condition, 59 per cent conformed at least once, 28 per cent yielded 3 to 12 times. Among participants in the control condition, 27 per cent erred at least once, 3.3 per cent made more than three errors. The differences between the experimental and control groups was significant. Thus this shows that a degree of conformity to a unanimous peer-group opinion remains observable. Participants reported considerable distress under the group pressure. This provides recent and powerful support for Asch's original result. This was also true of Boen et al. (2006), who used a panel judgement task similar to that used in the popular television dance contest *Strictly Come Dancing*, and demonstrated conformity of opinion when the panel heard each other's feedback.

There are substantial cultural differences, leading Smith & Bond (1998) to characterise countries as either individualist (e.g. USA) or collectivist (e.g. Japan) – conformity being higher in collectivist societies where the group is considered more important than the individual.

Summary: norms and conformity to them are made socially in a culture. When cultures change, norms and conformity change too, and so do the results of Asch replications. Asch's study is very striking, but has **low reliability**. Every replication brings different results.

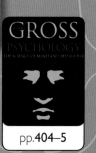

GROSS
PSYCHOLOGY
THE SCIENCE OF MIND AND BEHAVIOUR

pp.404–5

As well as the studies listed in 'Critical assessment'. This question **can** be answered by **also** using:
- comparison with studies in the 'context'
- criticisms from 'evaluation of method'.

Use at least **four** clear points or comparisons in total.

Procedure

Sample:

- 123 male college students were selected on a voluntary basis from four American universities.
- Each was paid $3 to participate in a study that involved a visual judgement task.

Design:

- They were tested in groups of seven to nine participants.
- Only one participant in each group was a real participant (the naive participant).
- The participant was seated sixth in a row of seven people.
- The others were **confederates** of Asch. (A confederate is a person who acts as if s/he is a participant but is really following the instructions of the experimenter.)
- Each group was shown two pieces of card. One had a 'standard' line printed on it; the other had three lines of varying length.

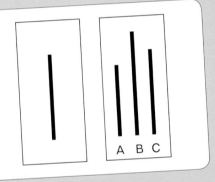

▲ **Figure 6.2**

- Each member of the group had to state aloud, in turn, which line they thought was the same length as the standard line.
- The true participant could see that one of the lines was obviously a match, the others obviously wrong.
- The answers were given in the order in which they were seated in the room, and on the first round every person chose the same line, which was the matching line.
- Then another set of cards was shown, and again the group was unanimous.
- On the third trial, and several later ones, the confederates unanimously gave the wrong answer.
- In all there were 18 trials, 12 of which were 'critical' in that the confederates deliberately gave wrong answers.

Findings

- In the control condition, where confederates gave the correct line each time, the naive participants answered correctly 98 per cent of the time (this gave Asch a baseline error rate).
- In the experimental condition, where the confederates gave the wrong answers, the naive participants were only correct in 63.2 per cent of cases.
- Participants conformed to the incorrect answer on 36.8 per cent of critical trials.
- 24 per cent of participants never conformed and gave their own answer.
- 5 per cent of participants conformed on all trials all of the time.
- 75 per cent of participants conformed at least once on critical trials.
- Participants were interviewed afterwards and asked why they conformed:

  - Distortion of perception — some participants believed the confederates were right.
  - Some participants wanted to please the researcher, and not 'spoil' the results.
  - Many of the participants thought they had a deficiency in themselves (e.g. poor eyesight), which they wanted to hide to avoid being laughed at.

Conclusions

- Some people will conform to group norms even when the answer is clearly wrong.
- This shows that conformity is a powerful influence on our behaviour.
- Asch (1955) said: 'That we have found the tendency to conformity in our society so strong that reasonably intelligent and well-meaning young people are willing to call white black is a matter of concern'.
- However, it is important to note that the participants remained independent on two-thirds of trials.
- Participants who did not follow the lead of the confederates held on to their own beliefs.

▲ **Figure 6.3** Some teenagers take up smoking to conform with their group of friends

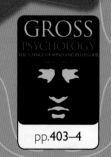

GROSS
PSYCHOLOGY
THE SCIENCE OF MIND AND BEHAVIOUR

pp.403–4

Evaluation of method – strengths and weaknesses

Design

✔ As this was a laboratory experiment it was conducted in **controlled conditions**. This allowed Asch to determine cause and effect when measuring conformity.

✘ The experiment lacked ecological validity – it is not very often in everyday life that people are asked to judge the length of a line against three other lines!

Sample

✔ The sample size of 123 participants was **large**.

✔ Using four different universities prevented participants being aware of the research purpose simply by word of mouth (**participant expectations**).

✔ The fact that they were all **similar in demographic details** (age, sex, etc.) means that they were with their peers. People are more likely to conform with peers in real life.

✔ The similarity in demographic details also means that potential **confounding variables** (e.g. gender differences) were removed from the experiment.

✘ Because the participants were all American males it may not be generalised to other groups, such as females or people in other cultures. This has been demonstrated to be important in subsequent research.

✘ The peer group demographic may also be a weakness, as perhaps Asch had weighted the results in the direction of conformity.

Ethics

✔ The participants were not able to give their fully **informed consent** as it would have been impossible to carry out the study if the participants had known the true nature of the experiment.

✔ Participants did not appear to suffer lasting **harm**.

✔ Participants were allowed to explain their actions in a **debrief**.

✗ Participants were subjected to a stressful situation and experienced temporary discomfort.

✗ No attempt was made to discover if lasting **damage** to self-esteem had occurred.

Reliability

✗ The results of other studies suggest that no standard method of measuring conformity works in every culture and therefore external reliability is low.

Validity

✗ Estimating line lengths is not a valid surrogate (substitute) for social opinions and attitudes.

▲ **Figure 6.4** As Asch's sample was made up of white American men, the results may not be generalisable to other groups

Context

Milgram was born in the Bronx, New York, to Jewish immigrants from Eastern Europe in 1933. Although his family was not particularly religious, they were deeply conscious of their roots and heritage, while remaining patriotic Americans. His family was profoundly affected by the Second World War, with many relatives suffering in the pogroms and the Holocaust. By his high-school days, Milgram was worried that the genocidal activities of the Nazis could be repeated in another country, so much so that his classmate Phillip Zimbardo described it as a near-obsession (Blass 2004).

▲ **Figure 6.5** The gates of Auschwitz - Milgram wanted to find out whether Nazi atrocities could be repeated in another country

Psychological explanations of the actions of 'ordinary' Germans varied from abnormal personality to amoral managerial behaviour. Adorno (1950) identified an '**authoritarian personality**', who obeyed orders from superiors but treated supposed inferiors in a rigid and destructive way. This was supposed to stem from a cold and punitive upbringing. This suggested something special in the Germanic character that led itself to unquestioning obedience. However, this was contradicted by Arendt (1963), who saw the operators of the death camps as managers who had lost their morality. She coined the memorable phrase '**the banality [ordinariness] of evil**'. Milgram tended to believe, like Arendt, that it was the **situation**, not the personality, that turned ordinary people into killers.

Milgram chose a career in social psychology late in his education and was research assistant to Asch. He went on to conduct cross-cultural **conformity experiments** comparing Americans and Norwegians, and then turned the methods he had developed to research into obedience.

He was a member of a loose group of '**Situationists**', including Zimbardo, who emphasised the power of situations in creating behaviour. As a radical social psychologist, his experiment was a distortion of the behaviourist conditioning scenario, where behaviour is rewarded or punished.

Aim

The aim of the study is to see if an authority figure can make ordinary citizens apparently injure others, simply by the power of the situation they find themselves in. This would then challenge the hypothesis that some character defect in Germans made obedience to authority unquestioning and total.

To learn more about situationists see http://thesituationist.wordpress.com

Critical assessment

Milgram went on to complete 16 more studies, all but one with a male sample, varying the conditions experimentally. The first major variation involved changing the distance between the 'teacher' and the 'learner' (**proximity condition**). He found that the closer the two, the lower the duration of shocks given. Introducing a defiant 'learner' also reduced the level of shock. There is a link here to the theory that deindividuation leads to aggression (as in Zimbardo's prison study) and that humanising a situation leads to diminished aggression. This supports his original work and also links to conformity research, especially the work of Moscovici on minority influence, where a dissident minority significantly alters group behaviour.

Milgram then introduced other (fake) teachers, and obedience plummeted when they refused to continue (down to 10 per cent). He then moved the studies to an office in a nearby town, thus removing the effect of a prestigious university location. Obedience levels here were lower than in the first series (47.5 per cent went to 450 volts), but not by much. Finally, he repeated the original conditions for a documentary film made of the obedience studies – the footage you often see on the internet or in documentaries. He was varying the situation and observing behavioural changes as a result – this was what Milgram expected, as a Situationist. Therefore the variation in results further strengthens both his basic theory and his ideological position.

Milgram's study was replicated by 17 other research groups, using the basic protocol, up to 1985. The mean obedience level (continue to 450v) was almost identical to Milgram's (65 per cent), with the highest rates found in the USA (Ring et al. 1970) at 91 per cent, and the lowest in Australia (Kilham & Mann 1974) at 28 per cent. The next lowest rates were found also in the USA in 1974. The BBC repeated the study for a 2009 documentary, obtaining 75 per cent going to 450v from a small sample. This suggests the phenomenon in general to be enduring and somewhat stable, but there is clearly a cultural effect at work, although the actual pattern is not clear.

Obedience to those in uniform in other situations have been demonstrated by a student of Milgram's asking people to give up their train seat (Takooshian 1972), and by Bickman (1974) telling people to pick up litter in New York. Hofling (1966) used a real-life hospital to demonstrate that most nurses will issue a dangerous dose of a drug on the orders of a doctor. All these studies provide convincing support for Milgram's position.

Obedience to those in authority is clearly consistent and present across cultures and time (Blass 2004; Zimbardo 2007) and indicates a persistent behavioural pattern in humans.

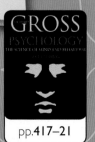

As well as the studies listed in 'Critical assessment'. This question **can** be answered by **also** using:
● comparison with studies in the 'context'
● criticisms from 'evaluation of method'.
Use at least **four** clear points or comparisons in total.

pp.417–21

Procedure

Sample:

- A self-selected sample, collected via newspaper adverts.
- 40 males aged between 20 and 50.
- They were from blue- and white-collar jobs and were paid $4.00 plus 50 cents for travel expenses (well above minimum wages in the early 1960s).

Design:

- The study was conceived as a pretend **memory experiment**, the actual focus being the behaviour that demonstrated the obedience of the participant.
- Two non-actors were hired to play the parts of 'experimenter' and 'learner'. The 'experimenter' dressed in a grey lab coat and was suitably severe in manner. The 'reality' of the pretence was enhanced by a **rigged draw** for 'teacher' and 'learner' roles, and also by a specimen shock given to the 'teacher'. The participant was always the 'teacher'.
- The teacher left the 'learner' strapped into a chair with electric shock equipment, seemingly ready to give them shocks during the study. The 'teacher' moved to another room where they sat at an instrument panel, supervised by the 'experimenter'.
- The shock apparatus had switches ascending from 15v to 450v, labelled with descriptions of intensity such as 'strong shock'; the final 435v and 450v switches had a label of 'XXXX'.
- The 'teacher' had to read out a list of pairs of words, and then the test phase would begin. The 'teacher' would read out the first word on the list and wait for the 'learner' to identify the appropriate, supposedly learnt, response words from a group of four, using one of four lights on a display. If the response was incorrect, a shock had to be delivered. On each incorrect response, the level of shock administered rose by one increment (switch).
- The 'learner' responses were all in fact scripted to occur identically in every trial. In the case of screams and demands, these were all pre-recorded and played at the same points in every trial.
- The 'experimenter' used scripted prompts or 'prods', such as, 'The experiment requires that you continue.'
- There was a final 'prod': 'Whether the learner likes it or not, you must go on until he has learnt all the word pairs correctly.'
- When all the prods had been used and the 'teacher' continued to refuse to continue, the trial was ended.
- If the 'teacher' went up to 450v they had to complete two more trials before the experiment was finished.
- Milgram obtained estimates of what (average) maximum voltage would be used from various groups during 1962:

  - Psychiatrists: 120v
  - Students: 150v
  - Middle-class adults: 135v

▲ **Figure 6.6** Milgram's shock generator

Findings

Quantitative:

- Five participants quit at 300v.
- Another nine quit by 375v (making 14 in total).
- 26/40 completed the full trial, giving 450v.

Qualitative:

- Most participants showed signs of emotional disturbance during and after the experiment.
- Some participants trembled, sweated, laughed nervously and showed signs of severe stress.
- Three participants appeared to have some form of fit, with one being so convulsive the experiment was stopped.
- Most participants questioned the experimenter constantly, often with great anxiety.
- A small number showed no emotion whatsoever.

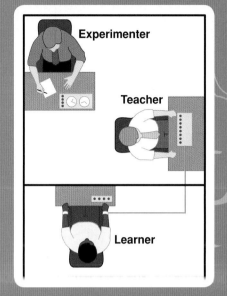

▲ **Figure 6.7** The layout of Milgram's laboratory

▲ **Figure 6.8** People are socialised to obey authority figures

Conclusions

Obedience occurred because:

- Participants were volunteers, so felt obliged to continue with the experiment. Participants became 'trapped' in the situation, torn between their obedience and their conscience (called '**entrapment**').
- The experimenter was a legitimate authority figure and people are socialised to obey such figures. Milgram theorised that participants moved from an autonomous state (normal) to an **agentic state** (under command and obeying orders).
- The experimenter took responsibility for events, which took away moral responsibility from the participants (**diffusion of responsibility**).
- The experiment was sited at Yale University, a top university in the USA – prestigious, official, scientific and conferring **legitimacy**.

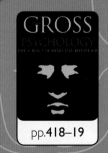

GROSS
PSYCHOLOGY
THE SCIENCE OF MIND AND BEHAVIOUR

pp.418–19

Evaluation of method – strengths and weaknesses

Design

✔ **Observation with experimental features**, not a formal experiment

✔ The **series of studies** constituted an experimental **design**

Sample

✔ A **typical** small American town sample

✔ **Volunteers** tend to be less authoritarian than others (Rosenthal & Rosnow 1966), so effect of procedure more striking

✔ The all-male sample was deliberately chosen to remove one possible **confounding variable** – gender (Milgram did 17 experiments using 636 participants; variation 8 included 40 females)

✘ Sample **unrepresentative** of Americans in general

✘ Sample was entirely male, so Milgram was accused of gender bias

Ethics

✔ Level of obedience was **not anticipated** in pre-study consultations

Milgram gave them:

✔ a **thorough debrief** in which they met the 'learner' and the 'experimenter'

✔ **questionnaire** about their experiences

✔ **counselling** support available for a year afterwards

✔ the way he dealt with the ethics in his experiment was not only **approved** by the American Psychological Association after investigation, but brought into their Code of Ethics

✘ Clear levels of distress shown by participants suggest that **protection** was not fully given

Reliability

✔ Milgram's method (**protocol**) has proved robust over time and between cultures, so highly reliable

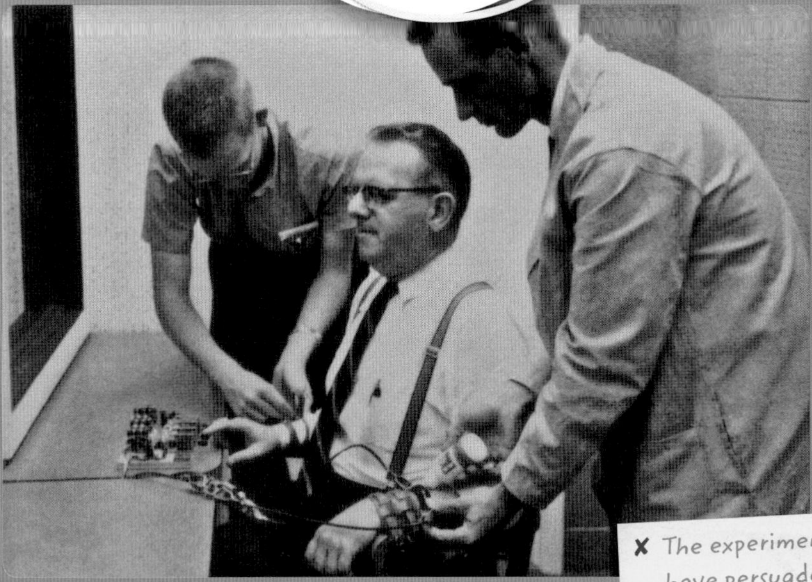

▲ **Figure 6.9**

Validity

✔ One line of argument is that the participants did not believe the scenario was real. If so, then why did they show such clear signs of emotional distress?

✖ The experimental situation could have persuaded participants to hope that no harm was really being done, so they were more likely to continue (low ecological validity)

✖ Did the experiment lack mundane realism as it was not a lifelike situation?

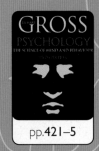

GROSS
PSYCHOLOGY
THE SCIENCE OF MIND AND BEHAVIOUR

pp.421–5

Context

Anything that happens in a person's environment causes some form of reaction in the body (General Adaptation Syndrome). Persistent events cause long-term physical and psychological effects (which we call stress). The drain on the body's resources following continued stress causes damage to the immune system and makes people more likely to get infections or other physical illnesses, as well as psychological states such as depression.

Rosenman & Friedman (1950) found a link between stress and subsequent heart disease. They identified a type of personality that had damaging reactions to stress (**Type A personality**).

One problem is the difficulty of measuring preceding stress and linking it with subsequent ill-health. There were no established ways of quantifying stress except by self-reports. Thomas Holmes and Richard Rahe developed existing life-event measurement scales that they tested in various forms during the late 1960s and early 1970s. They were pioneers of a new approach to stress testing. The Schedule of Recent Experiences (SRE) was the original test (Holmes & Hawkins 1957) that was used in its developed form by Rahe in this study.

A large sample of ordinary people rated the relative impact of a list of life events presented to them by the researchers. The ratings were then averaged and converted into a set of standardised scores, where 'death of a spouse' rated 100, and all other events proportionately less. This list was then used to try to predict ill-health by getting individuals to add up their recent life-event scores and then see if they became ill. This is actually very difficult to do in a valid manner in real life!

Many of the studies were retrospective, using people who were already in hospital and looking back over their recent lives – this method is very prone to errors of recall (e.g. Rahe 1964). A **prospective** study, which looks at data that emerge from the present onwards, is not subject to this.

Rahe was a medical student when he worked with Holmes (a psychiatrist) and is a qualified doctor who specialises in stress-related medical problems. He worked for the US Navy for 20 years, and this study was part of a massive research programme funded in the 1960s and 1970s by the Navy (as was Zimbardo's prison study). The US Navy wanted to understand how people reacted in closed environments (e.g. on board an operational craft), how specific environments affected behaviour, and how better management of those environments could affect health and behaviour.

Aim

To investigate the impact of life events, as measured by a life-stress test (SRE) on health, in serving US Navy personnel, using a prospective research design.

Definitions

1. Retrospective design i measure variable 2, then look backwards in time to try to measure variable 1.

2. Prospective design i measure variable 1, then wait for a period of time and measure variable 2.

Critical assessment

The Social Readjustment Rating Scale (SRRS) was tested with several samples of US populations and with Asian groups in Japan and South East Asia (Holmes & Masuda 1973). It became an established stress test and is a good predictor of psychological and physical illness (Miller 1989).

However, one of the major criticisms of the life-event approach was that many people do not experience these major events, yet seem to get stress-related illness. Goldberg & Comstock (1980) found that 15 per cent of a sample of 2,800 adults had not experienced any of the listed life events in the preceding year. This suggests that the link between stress and ill-health is not as straightforward as Holmes & Rahe's study suggests.

There is certainly a clear link for types of cancer. Palesh et al. (2007) found that relapses in breast cancer patients were linked to stressful life events, and there are links for other conditions such as heart disease (Abraham et al. 2008). However, a major confounding issue is that some life events (e.g. loss of employment) may be symptoms of a developing illness (Penny 1996), and many overviews of the field conclude that linking evidence in general is weak (Abraham 2008).

The life-events list itself is not only well out of date (Lazarus 1999), but it does not take the context of the life event into account (Forshaw 2002). A divorce may be a positive event for one or both people concerned. This suggests that Holmes & Rahe's finding is out of date.

Kanner (1981) suggested it was the minor stressors of day-to-day life that had a bigger effect on health overall. A scale was developed to measure this, which Kanner called the Hassles and Uplifts Scale. This was based on the idea that good events could have a positive effect on health as well. The Hassles Scale was a better predictor of psychological health than Holmes & Rahe's SRRS.

Research has suggested that there is a substantial cumulative effect of hassles (Almeida 2005) and it is likely that hassles disrupt healthy lifestyles, disrupt self-care procedures and make existing symptoms worse with the increased release of stress hormones (Gross 2010).

Because everyone experiences a stressor in different ways, a Perceived Stress Scale was developed (Cohen 1986). This has been extensively used in the late twentieth century and the early twenty-first, because it has been easily modified for different cultures and does not rely on specific life events to measure stress, unlike the relatively culture-bound SRRS.

Despite the considerable limitations of the approach developed by Holmes & Rahe, the number of studies increases every decade (Dohrenwend 2006).

As well as the studies listed in 'Critical assessment'.
This question **can** be answered by **also** using:
- comparison with studies in the 'context'
- criticisms from 'evaluation of method'.
Use at least **four** clear points or comparisons in total.

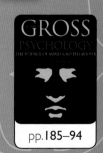

GROSS
PSYCHOLOGY
THE SCIENCE OF MIND AND BEHAVIOUR

pp.185–94

Procedure

Sample:

- All-male sample of serving US Navy personnel (women not allowed on the front line at that time).
- 2,664 men on three carriers on active service.
- Average age was 22.3.
- Two-thirds of the men were high school graduates.
- Length of service ranged up to 30 years.
- Sample represented over 90 per cent of the men on the ships.

▲ **Figure 7.1**

Design:

- A double-blind study in that neither the sample nor the staff analysing medical records knew the purpose of the study.
- A modified version of SRRS (SRE) completed every 6 months over a period of 2 years.
- Life Change Units score (LCU) was calculated from the established questionnaire (SRRS).
- Followed by a tour of duty of 6 to 8 months.
- All illnesses were recorded on ship's medical files.
- Medical records were then scrutinised and assessed independently of the researcher by medical staff, and a health score compiled using number, type and severity of illness.
- Any participants with previously known conditions were not used, nor were those who were reported to be faking or shirking work.

Analysis:

- LCU scores were banded (1 to 10) and grouped – the higher the LCU band, the higher the mean illness rating.
- LCU scores and health scores were correlated.

Findings

LCU bands	Mean illness score
1 + 2	1.405
3 + 4 + 5	1.541
6 + 7 + 8	1.676
9 + 10	2.066

- The only positive correlation was between LCU (6 months prior to cruise) and medical score.
- + 0.118 is high for such a large sample.
- The higher the LCU score, the higher the mean illness rate.
- The highest LCU scores (195–1,000) — a small minority — had much higher illness rates than the majority (0–194).
- There was a clear relationship between TLCU (total life change unit) score and later illness rates.
- Both TLCU scores and illness rates were low relative to a general population.
- More accurate predictive power in older sailors than younger.
- The strongest correlation between LCU scores and illness rates was found on the two ships that did not see action.

Conclusions

- Higher LCU scores in the 6 months prior to departure were associated with **higher illness rates** during the tour of duty.
- The **link was stronger** for older men and married men.
- The life-event approach **correctly predicted** a significant correlation between LCU score and illness rate (**predictive validity**).

▲ **Figure 7.2** Stress makes people vulnerable to physical illnesses

Evaluation of methodology – strengths and weaknesses

Design

✔ This was **prospective,** not retrospective (a much more powerful and valid design)

✔ Restricted environment enables **control** and scrutiny of all **variables**

✔ **Double-blind study** reduces **demand characteristics** to a minimum

Sample

✔ Relatively **homogeneous** sample

✔ Reduction in number of **extraneous variables** (e.g. gender, gender interactions)

✔ **Opportunity sample,** easy to acquire once permission was granted!

✔ It was customary for crew to report even minor illnesses, so **data were comprehensive**

✗ Biased sample: Rahe suggests that in a more normal population the correlation between the two variables would probably be larger, as the sample was very fit people with heightened resistance to illness

Ethics

✔ Once permission was granted by the US Navy Command there were **no issues with consent or deception,** as the Navy held those permissions, not the men

Validity

✔ **Prospective** design provides valid and largely uncontaminated data

✔ Showed very clear positive correlation between stress score (TLCU) and illness frequency, showing TLCU is a valid test (**high predictive validity**)

✘ Confounding factor was combat stress, which tended to obscure other stresses (cruiser 2)

◀ **Figure 7.3** The Navy personnel were all fit; in the general population the relationship between stress and illness might be even stronger

Reliability

✔ The medical records were **comprehensive and systematic**, so the method was highly **reliable**

✘ The reliability of self-reporting of stress is questionable; people tend to change their reports over time (Raphael et al. 1991)

Context

Phobias are irrational fears. The emergence of phobias between four and five years of age without obvious precipitating experiences suggests that a genetic component is at work.

Evidence comes from a number of surveys of fears and phobias (e.g. Agras et al. 1969; Costello 1982; Kirkpatrick 1984) to show consistent and widespread patterns of fear focused on a small number of stimuli. These included animals, particularly snakes and spiders, as well as heights, thunder, fire, deep water and death. These fears all appear to have **evolutionary significance** in that each would have represented survival threats to people. Mineka et al. (1980) showed a fear of moving snakes in laboratory-raised monkeys that had never seen snakes, suggesting a **genetic origin** for the fears. Those who had a genetic predisposition to learn rapidly to associate snakes with danger were more likely to avoid snakes, and live to successfully reproduce. This predisposition to **anxiety** thus became more and more common in human groups. Similar effects occurred with other stimuli, including spiders, fire, deep water and so on.

This '**biological preparedness**' hypothesis is particularly associated with Seligman (1970) and includes the expression of disgust and avoidance of objects with poisonous characteristics (e.g. discoloured meat, bad smells).

One alternative hypothesis is that humans were prepared to learn to be frightened by powerful, sudden or new events in general, and that when animals showed such characteristics (e.g. big, quick and has teeth), then fear was quickly generalised. This hypothesis has support from the **General Adaptation Syndrome** (GAS), where the alarm stage is triggered by any unanticipated event in the environment.

A final hypothesis is Hinde's (1974) **theory of discrepancy**: we fear the strangeness of an animal, and the more strange or unfamiliar (discrepant) it is, the greater the initial fear.

Aim

Bennett-Levy & Marteau set out to test whether the anxiety was actually related to the animals most frequently feared, or whether it was some general attributes that the animals displayed (e.g. making sudden movements) that triggered fear. This is testing Seligman's 'preparedness' hypothesis.

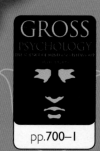

GROSS
PSYCHOLOGY

pp.700–1

Critical assessment

Bennett-Levy & Marteau's results challenge Seligman's 'preparedness' hypothesis as they suggest it is stimulus characteristics that are relevant, not the type of animal. The most feared animals are the 'ugliest' and those with antennae, tentacles and so on, which supports Hinde's discrepancy hypothesis.

Some laboratory studies suggest that fear is acquired more readily with the 'traditional' stimuli (e.g. snakes and spiders) than with less feared stimuli (e.g. Mineka 1987; Ohman & Soares 1998) and that it is also more resistant to extinction (e.g. McNally 1987), but they also showed that evidence for rapid acquisition was very mixed. Some studies seemed to show powerful evidence (e.g. Ihman 1979), but many others showed weak fear learning that was easily reversed. These results are clearly not reliable.

Clinical studies look at groups of individual cases. First, these studies have not always confirmed that prepared fears represent the majority of clinical fears. Studies such as de Silva (1988) support this hypothesis, but Merckelbach *et al.* (1988) found that most of the clinical phobias in their sample were not of the 'prepared' type. This study did find, however, that 'prepared' type fears were much harder to treat. In general, clinical studies have not supported Seligman's 'preparedness' hypothesis.

Studies using laboratory-bred primates – who had never seen snakes – did show that fear of snakes is more easily acquired than fear of flowers (Cook & Mineka 1989). However, a major criticism is that many monkeys learn fear and associated behaviours from older monkeys, and they are very sensitive to the experimenter's reactions, especially to live snakes (Cheney & Seyfarth 1990).

Mormann *et al.* (2011) used a sample of 41 volunteers with epilepsy, so they could use direct electrode recording from brain structures. They found that there was an automatic arousal response to the appearance (picture) of an animal detectable in the amygdala of humans. This was not modified by whether the animal was threatening or not. So this suggests that 'preparedness' is for recognition of animals in general and not for any characteristics or threat potential.

Overall, there is little evidence to support Seligman's 'preparedness' hypothesis, but much to support the hypothesis that it is general attributes that promote fear. One example is fear of flying, for which there is no evolutionary explanation; however; the attributes of speed and powerlessness are clearly major factors in the development of extreme fear.

As well as the studies listed in 'Critical assessment'.
This question **can** be answered by **also** using:
- comparison with studies in the 'context'
- criticisms from 'evaluation of method'.
Use at least **four** clear points or comparisons in total.

Procedure

Sample:

- The sample consisted of 113 people attending a local health clinic in Britain.
- Each person completed either questionnaire 1 or questionnaire 2.
- Allocation to groups was random.
- In both groups the numbers of males and females were approximately equal and the mean age was very similar (just over 35 years).
- Questionnaire 1 – 34 females and 30 males, mean age 35.5 years.
- Questionnaire 2 – 25 females and 24 males, mean age 35.1 years.

Data collection: the study used self-report questionnaires.

Questionnaire 1:

- This was a self-report measure of fear and avoidance of 29 small, harmless animals.
- It was made clear that the animals were harmless in captions next to the pictures.
- Participants rated the animals on two scales:
    - Fear scale – rated on a 3-point scale (1 = not afraid, 3 = very afraid)
    - Nearness – rated their avoidance on a 5-point scale (1 = enjoy picking up, 5 = move further away than 2 metres).

Questionnaire 2:

- This measured the participants' perceptions in relation to the same animals as in questionnaire 1.
- They were asked to rate each on a 3-point rating (1 = not, 2 = quite, 3 = very).
- The characteristics they rated were:
    - ugly
    - slimy
    - speedy
    - how suddenly they appear to move.

▲ **Figure 7.4**

Findings

- Gender differences in the results showed that females were less likely to pick up ten of the species than were males (including the jellyfish, cockroach, spider and slug).
- There were no gender differences in ratings of ugliness, sliminess, speediness or suddenness of movement.
- Speediness and suddeness of movement were highly correlated.
- More complex analysis showed that speedy or suddenly moving animals were less likely to be approached closely and elicited greater fear.
- Ugliness was related to nearness — 'ugly' animals were less likely to be approached closely.
- 'Sliminess' was related to fear — the more slimy the animal, the more fear elicited.

Variables correlated	Correlation
Speedy/sudden movement	0.95
Nearness/fear	0.95
Ugly/nearness	0.87
Ugly/fear	0.82
Slimy/nearness	0.77
Slimy/fear	0.61
Ugly/slimy	0.75

Conclusions

- Although **perceived harmfulness** is one factor in eliciting fear, other factors are also important.
- **Perceptual characteristics** (ugly, slimy, speedy and sudden movement) contribute greatly to fear elicitation.
- The most feared animals are the 'ugliest' and those with antennae, tentacles and so on, which **supports Hinde's discrepancy hypothesis**.
- The 'preparedness' hypothesis relating to specific animals has **little support**.

▲ Figure 7.5

Evaluation of methodology – strengths and weaknesses

✔ **Simple method** that can provide results speedily

✔ **Separation of questionnaires** prevents expectations developing in participants, so response patterns not due to **demand characteristics**

Design

✘ Correlation demonstrates association but not cause and effect. Therefore while the ugly/fear correlation is high (0.82), it does not mean that ugliness is a factor in causing fear

✘ Questionnaire method lacks **ecological validity** in relation to the subject matter of the investigation – asking people about pictures is not the same as seeing the actual animal

✘ Some **participants' perceptions** over-ruled the 'harmless' captions

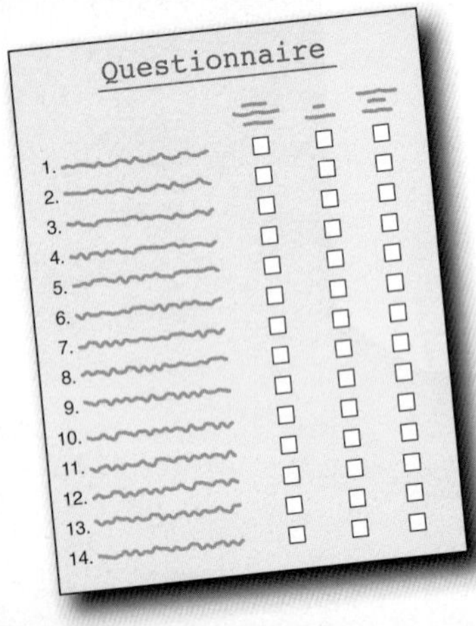

▲ **Figure 7.6** Using questionnaires avoided demand characteristics but may have lacked ecological validity

✘ Sample is quite **small**

✘ Sample is relatively **monocultural**, so does not reflect other cultures

✘ No **control sample** from cultures where target animals live naturally (e.g. poisonous snakes are numerous)

Sample

✔ Contains both males and females, so can allow for **gender differences** if they occur

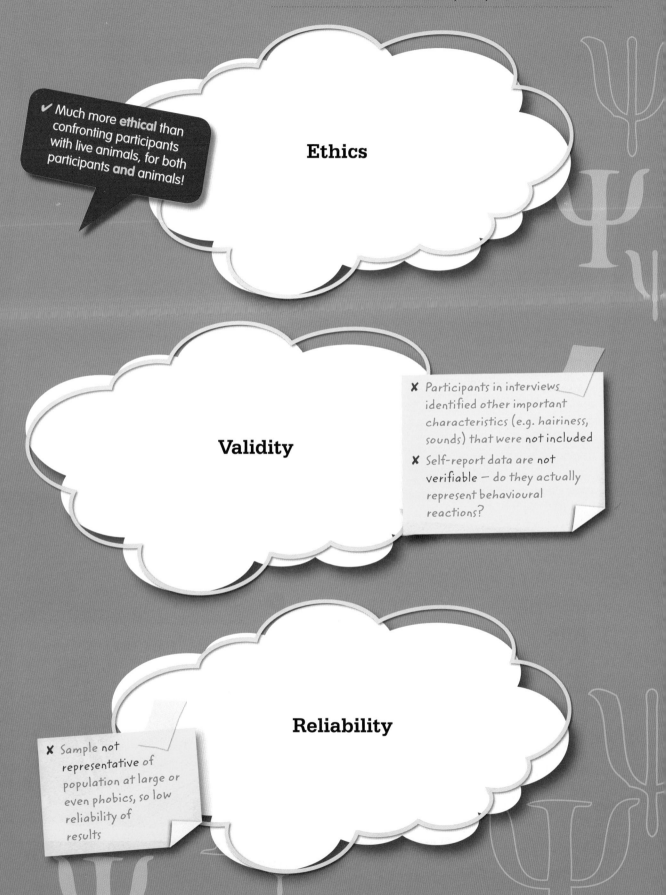

Ethics

✔ Much more **ethical** than confronting participants with live animals, for both participants **and** animals!

Validity

✗ Participants in interviews identified other important characteristics (e.g. hairiness, sounds) that were not included

✗ Self-report data are not verifiable — do they actually represent behavioural reactions?

Reliability

✗ Sample not representative of population at large or even phobics, so low reliability of results

Context

The nature of memory as a reconstruction, rather than a reproduction, was explored by Bartlett (1932). He demonstrated that we use our experience to reconstruct aspects of the past, and distort these according to our beliefs and stereotypes. In one of his more famous designs, he used both pictures and texts to explore successive reproduction – better known as 'Chinese whispers'.

People actively try to make sense of the fragments of their memories, and will unconsciously **incorporate** elements of their attitudes (especially stereotypes), **conflate** them with similar events from the past, or even **confabulate** (invent aspects of the event to enable the memory to make sense).

Recall can be influenced by previous events (**proactive interference**) and by subsequent events (**retroactive interference**). Early evidence for retroactive interference comes from learning two sets of connected words (set A to set B, then set A to set C). Inevitably, the A–C link blocks the previously learnt A–B link (Barnes & Underwood 1959). This means that new learning may alter the old information – such as clues and hints you unconsciously pick up when you are asked about an event in the past. An example might be the effect of a question (such as 'What did the suspect look like?' as opposed to 'What did the man look like?'). Eyewitness identification can be distorted or replaced with a false identification.

Loftus originally became interested in memory towards the end of her postgraduate course, but did not turn to eyewitness testimony until she decided to combine her psychology research with her interest in real-life crime. Radin (1964) estimated that false convictions in the USA, based on eyewitness testimony, were as high as 5 per cent, and were one of the biggest causes of wrongful conviction. Many of these false convictions were subsequently exposed by DNA testing, but unfortunately many of the defendants had already been executed! In the UK, eyewitness testimony has normally to be supported by other forms of evidence, and appeals are possible since the UK has no death penalty. Her research into reconstructive memory uses the mechanism for retroactive interference to alter eyewitness recall, simply by a small change in the question asked by an interviewer.

Aim

The aim of Loftus's studies was to see if a single word change in a subsequent interview question can have a material effect on recall of an event (eyewitness testimony). The first study aimed to see if a change in wording caused a change in speed estimate. The second study aimed to see if the questioning altered the memory stored.

▲ **Figure 8.1** In the UK, eyewitness testimony must be supported by other evidence

Critical assessment

Loftus (1997) has subsequently demonstrated that **false memories** can be created in virtually any case by the use of misleading suggestion. This has been of vital importance where '**recovered memories**' from therapy have led to abuse prosecutions many years after the supposed event, with no other supporting evidence.

Real-life evidence of the false memory effect comes from the USA. The Oklahoma City bombing in 1995, where white supremacists bombed a Federal building and killed 168 people, resulted in the conviction of Timothy McVeigh. Memon & Wright (1999) studied the eyewitness accounts, and found that a witness described two men renting a truck, one being McVeigh. It turned out that he had seen the other man renting a truck the day before, but the memories had become fused together. Following the initial news reports of the second man, existing witnesses started to recall him, despite having not reported him initially – two real-life examples of false memory.

These studies suggest that there can be considerable scepticism about the accuracy of eyewitness testimony, supporting Loftus's thesis

The **ecological validity** of the Loftus & Palmer study has been a source of much research:

- When witnessing real-life events, in this case bank robberies, Christianson & Hubinette (1993) showed that recall was both accurate and stayed so for up to 15 months.
- This was even true of laboratory studies, where the participants were told that the robbery on video was real and their responses would influence the trial (Foster 1994).
- Yuille & Cutshill (1986) found extremely good recall after a real shooting, despite high levels of stress.

This evidence does not support Loftus's study, as it suggests that in real life memory is far more accurate.

Further evidence is also contradictory:

- Misleading information, such as the content of a question, does not usually affect central detail of a witness account (Read & Bruce 1984).
- Real-life studies show that the more emotional arousal that occurs, the better the memory for central details (Yuille & Cutshill 1986).
- Loftus herself (1979) showed that blatantly incorrect misinformation had no effect on recall of key details when she attempted to alter recall of the colour of a victim's bag during a street robbery scenario.
- However, Loftus showed that memory for events with a weapon (**weapon effect**) is much poorer than for events without a weapon involved (Loftus 1987).
- The questions asked in the standard Loftus experiment do not seem to lead to permanent changes in memory, only temporary alterations at the time (Zaragoza et al. 1987).
- An overview of studies concluded that identification accuracy does not decrease with time (Hewstone et al. 2005).

Thus evidence is somewhat chaotic and contradictory and therefore exhibits very low reliability.

Loftus's study has received both support and refutation over a period of 30 years. However, in the UK, police interview practice was affected, with careful scrutiny of questioning, increased use of neutral questioning and increased use of the cognitive interview, all designed to reduce false memory effects.

As well as the studies listed in 'Critical assessment'.
This question **can** be answered by **also** using:
- comparison with studies in the 'context'
- criticisms from 'evaluation of method'.

Use at least **four** clear points or comparisons in total.

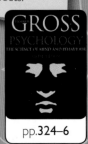

GROSS
PSYCHOLOGY
THE SCIENCE OF MIND AND BEHAVIOUR

pp.324–6

Procedure

▲ **Figure 8.2**

Experiment 1

Sample:

- The sample – 45 students (five groups of nine students in an **independent measures design**).

Design:

- The procedure – the students watched film clips of car accidents.
- After watching the films, the students were asked to do **two** things: 1. Write an account of what they had seen. 2. Answer questions about what they had seen.
- One question was the **critical question**: 'About how fast were the cars going when they _____ each other.'
- There were five conditions (verbs) in the experiment.
- The five **conditions** (verbs) were:

  - contacted
  - hit
  - bumped
  - smashed
  - collided.

Experiment 2

Sample:

- The participants – 150 students (three groups of 50 students in an independent measures design).

Design:

- Students watched a 1-minute film, which showed a 4-second, multiple car accident.
- After the film the participants were divided into three experimental groups.

  - Group 1 was asked: 'How fast were the cars going when they **hit** each other?'
  - Group 2 was asked: 'How fast were the cars going when they **smashed into** each other?'
  - Group 3 was not asked a question about the speed of the cars.

One week later the participants returned and were asked more questions:

A)   The critical question

B)   'Did you see any broken glass?'

Findings
Experiment 1

Verb used in critical question	Average speed estimate (mph)
smashed	40.8
collided	39.3
bumped	38.1
hit	34.0
contacted	31.8

- There was a direct relationship between the **verb used** in the critical question and the **average estimate of speed** given by the participants.
- The actual speed of the vehicle bore no relationship to the estimates given.

Experiment 2

Probability of 'yes' answer to 'broken glass' question:

Verb used in critical question	Speed estimate	
	11–15 mph	16–20 mph
'smashed'	41%	62%
'hit'	25%	50%

- Speed estimates were likely to be higher in the 'smashed' condition.
- This was reflected in the likelihood of a 'yes' answer to the 'broken glass' question.

	'smashed'	'hit'	Control group
Yes	16	7	6
No	34	43	44

- Most participants did not recall seeing any broken glass.
- The recall rate in the 'smashed' condition was twice that of the 'hit' condition.
- The 'control' condition had a similar recall rate to 'hit', which suggests a general false memory rate; the 'smashed' condition was significantly different.

Conclusions
Experiment 1:
- The format of a post-event interview question can **significantly affect** a witness's answer.
- This may constitute a form of **'bias'** to recall, **or**
- It may mean there has been an alteration to the actual memory.

Experiment 2:
- Memories formed at the time of the event become **mixed up** with further information post-event.
- These two sets of information become fused together and constitute an **altered memory**.

NOTE: When quoting the findings, the **exact** figures are needed in all tables to gain the highest marks.

▲ **Figure 8.3** The participants were asked whether they remembered seeing any broken glass

Evaluation of methodology – strengths and weaknesses

Design

- ✔ Standard laboratory experiment
- ✔ High degree of control
- ✔ Cause and effect easy to determine

- ✘ Use of video rather than real-life event, coupled with laboratory setting, means that ecological validity could be very low
- ✘ Complete lack of mundane realism, as car crashes take place without prior expectation – that is, witnesses are not expecting it!

Sample

- ✔ Relatively **homogeneous** since students tend to be of the same age and educational level

- ✘ Students are notoriously unrepresentative of the population at large on many variables (age, educational level, socio-economic origin, attitudes and values, etc.)
- ✘ No control in sampling for those with driving experience (which may inform estimates of speed)

Ethics

- ✔ Virtually **no ethical problems** as consent obtained, minimal deception, students unlikely to be upset by a video car crash and post-study information was available

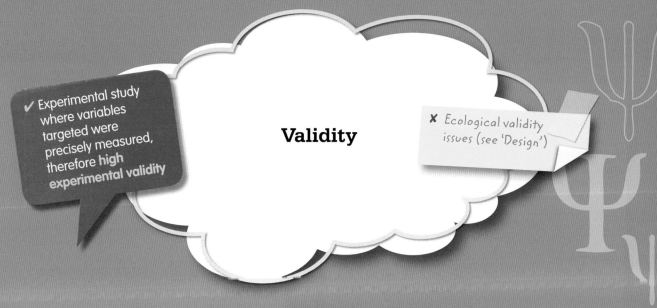

Validity

✔ Experimental study where variables targeted were precisely measured, therefore **high experimental validity**

✗ Ecological validity issues (see 'Design')

▲ **Figure 8.4** Students are not necessarily representative of the wider population

✔ The effect of the video clips was shown to be **reliable** by the similar speed estimate relationships found in Experiments 1 and 2

Reliability

Context

Our communications use at least four separate systems – gesture and posture, facial expression, noise-making and language. Each of these systems on their own can convey meaning, and in the case of profoundly deaf people, the gesture system has been adapted (as sign language) to take the place of noise-making.

Language is the use of noises to communicate in a highly organised manner that extends the **referent** (thing being talked about) both into the past and into the future, and example is referring to things that are not physically present.

Linguists such as Chomsky (1957) theorised that humans alone had the biological programming to use language.

Humans have a distant common ancestor with chimpanzees (about 6 million years ago), but are still closely genetically related; we are another type of ape. There are millions of years of divergent evolution between us however, and despite clear intelligence, chimpanzees do not have natural language. They clearly are able to make gestures and noises as part of their natural communication, but can they be taught to demonstrate elements of language?

In the wild, chimps only vocalise in arousal, whether in excitement or threat situations. There are also severe limitations over the use of chimps – they become increasingly dangerous after the first three or four years as they are naturally very aggressive creatures (this is not the case for gorillas or bonobos).

Early attempts at teaching language to chimps (Kellogg & Kellogg 1933; Hayes 1950) were destined to fail, as they did not take into account physical differences – chimps cannot imitate human noises, because their vocal chords are different, and are located lower in the throat. The Hayes used operant conditioning to reward vocalisation, but their chimp Vicki only managed to vocalise four words. However, the Kelloggs' chimp, Gua, recognised and acted on about a hundred spoken words. This suggests that difficulties are in verbalising (production), not understanding (comprehension). When symbols were used instead of vocalisations (Premack & Premack 1966), the chimp, Sara, learnt over a hundred symbols, but did not use them to spontaneously communicate.

Most psychologists believed that language was the great barrier between humans and animals. The Gardners set out to investigate the truth of this in the first scientific investigation. They decided to use sign language, to mimic deaf human learning and to exploit the chimp's natural use of gesture and natural powers of imitation.

Aim

The Gardners intended to train a chimp in American Sign Language (ASL) from babyhood, and to scientifically document any growth in use. They expected to find some abilities in communication that had not been previously shown, including some aspects of language.

GROSS
PSYCHOLOGY
THE SCIENCE OF MIND AND BEHAVIOUR

pp.297–301

Critical assessment

The Gardners' research programme with Washoe was brought to a halt by the work of Terrace (1979). He alleged he had proved that his chimp Nim merely imitated the trainers and did not use ASL independently at all. This research was believed to refute the Gardners' conclusions.

The Gardners showed that Terrace's work was unscientific and sloppy, and more recent criticism has largely discredited him. However, their critics won the day and their project lost funding. This also happened to Patterson and her work with Koko the gorilla, although she was able to continue privately and show a considerable – if disputed – language capacity. The Gardners did eventually manage to start another project (Gardner 1989), demonstrating that chimps could use signs between themselves.

Dean Rumbaugh and Sue Savage had taken a different line, following the work of Premack & Premack (1966), who used symbols instead of gestures to teach a chimp. They created an electronic keyboard display (eventually portable) and also began to use bonobos (a different, rarer, type of chimp), as they were far less aggressive than common chimps.

Their work took off when they were training a female bonobo, Matata, who was raising a baby orphan. The orphan, Kanzi, merely observed the training as a baby, but began to show considerable ability independently. This research has developed into a major programme, with Kanzi and other bonobos showing understanding of spoken language, and being able to generate simple sentences using a portable computerised symbol board (Savage-Rumbaugh 2003). Kanzi has demonstrated over 2,000 non-imitative combinations of symbols (known as lexigrams).

The tasks given to Kanzi, Panbanisha and other bonobos involve them understanding the structure of sentences. Kanzi can distinguish between 'Put the ball on the pine needles' and 'Put the pine needles on the ball' by responding correctly. Testing follows a double-blind protocol (usually giving standard instructions via loudspeaker), so no cues can be accidentally given to the bonobos. Their research fully supports the Gardners' original hypothesis, that some elements of language could be acquired by chimps.

One interesting conclusion from the Rumbaughs' research is that bonobos are more adept at language than chimps, and there are considerable differences in ability between individuals – some never get the idea, others struggle, and some, like Kanzi, develop amazing ability. This suggests that the Gardners had an able chimp in Washoe.

Most scientists now accept that primates in general have considerable intellectual abilities, and that most of the elements of language are not exclusively human – indeed, some elements have been demonstrated by African Grey parrots (Pepperberg, 2007) as well as dolphins (Herman et al. 1984).

Ape 'language' seems to resemble early human acquisition (toddler age), especially signalling and requesting forms. While humans seem to be genetically prepared to acquire language, apes have a basic language capacity that can be developed. This raises the issue of the legal rights of these primates.

As well as the studies listed in 'Critical assessment'. This question **can** be answered by **also** using:
- comparison with studies in the 'context'
- criticisms from 'evaluation of method'.

Use at least **four** clear points or comparisons in total.

Procedure

Sample:

- Washoe, a female chimpanzee aged between 8 and 14 months at the start of the study, was the only participant.

Design:

- This was a **case study**.
- The focus for the first few months was establishing a daily routine and relationships between her carers, who worked in shifts to look after her.
- Her human companions were to be friends and playmates and introduce games and activities that would result in maximum interaction.
- All communication was restricted to ASL (American Sign Language), either with Washoe herself or with others in view of Washoe.

▲ **Figure 8.5** Washoe

Several techniques were used to teach Washoe:

- imitation – a researcher would show Washoe a gesture and if she imitated she was rewarded (being tickled)
- prompting – at times Washoe would lapse into poor 'diction' (using a sign sloppily); when this happened she was shown the correct sign and imitated once more
- using signs – all activities and objects were named with appropriate signs so she could associate the signs with everyday things
- babbling – babble is important in human language development, so Washoe was left to babble; when babbling occurred the babble was repeated back and linked to actual signs
- operant conditioning – rewards were used to increase the likelihood that behaviour would be repeated
- shaping – in the beginning Washoe was rewarded for producing a sign similar to the actual sign, but as time progressed she was only rewarded for producing the actual sign
- direct tuition – a teacher would form her hands into the correct gestures and then she would repeat this.

Data collection:

- Over the 22-month period, a record was kept of Washoe's language acquisition.
- Set criteria had to be fulfilled in order for a new sign to count as **acquired**:
  - three different researchers had to independently report seeing Washoe using the sign spontaneously and appropriately
  - the sign had to recorded throughout a 15-day period.

Findings

- Within 22 months Washoe had learnt 34 signs (meeting the Gardners' strict criteria).
- The earliest signs were simple demands, such as come-gimme, more, sweet.
- The later ones were mainly the names of objects, like baby, hat, shoes.
- Four other words were judged to be stable (dog, smell, me, clean), but these had not met the criteria.

Washoe's language resembles that of a human child in three ways:

- **differentiation** — some signs became differentiated, for example:
  - Washoe used 'more' largely to mean 'do it again' for an action she did not know the sign for, and 'flower' to mean smell (in response to the smell of tobacco).
  - She did learn a new sign for 'smell', although 'flower' was sometimes still used.
- **transfer** — signs such as 'more' and 'open' generalised readily from the original contexts to new ones, for example:
  - 'Flower' was applied not only to different flowers and contexts (indoors and outdoors), but also to pictures of flowers.
  - She was also able to sign 'dog' when she heard a dog barking but did not see it.
- **combination** — once Washoe had learnt a few signs she was able to combine two or three signs to represent more complex meanings, for example:
  - She used 'listen dog' in reference to a dog barking. This may have happened because the researchers were signing and Washoe may have just copied them.
  - However, she did produce some of her own combinations, such as 'open food door' (open the fridge) and 'go sweet' (to be carried to the raspberry bush).

Conclusions

- The findings suggest that **sign language was a good choice** for achieving two-way communication between humans and chimps.
- Washoe's expanding vocabulary, including nouns and verbs, her spontaneous transfer of meanings and combinations of signs all suggest that she was **intellectually capable** of acquiring signs and using them to communicate.
- However, the Gardners were **wary** of answering the question of whether Washoe had acquired language.
- They argued that this question **can only be answered** if there is a clear way to distinguish between one class of communicative behaviour that can be called a language and another class that cannot.

▲ **Figure 8.6**

Evaluation of methodology – strengths and weaknesses

Design

✔ The whole study was an **appropriate research design** (case study)

✔ Testing and recording were scientifically designed to be **sceptical** (i.e. difficult to falsify) – for example, the strict criteria for counting a sign as learnt by Washoe

✔ The **use of ASL** was appropriately founded on previous studies that had showed that gesture is normal for chimps, even laboratory-reared ones, and vocalisation, except under arousal, is not; human and chimp hands are similar

✔ Test observers were not aware of the context of a sign, so interpretation in testing was not contaminated (**observer bias**)

✘ Due to the termination of the project, most of the Gardners' data remain unanalysed.

Sample

✘ There was no check or comparison at that time of the normality of Washoe, so she may not have been typical of other chimps

Ethics

✔ Washoe had a **better life** than if she had been used for laboratory testing purposes

✘ Someone unknown had taken Washoe from her family and sold her (not the Gardners!)

✘ The Gardners largely kept her away from other chimps, which is cruel to an individual of an extremely social species

Validity

✔ This was a **far more valid and scientific** study than earlier ones

▲ **Figure 8.7** Gesture is normal for chimps

✔ The criteria for confirming the use of a sign are **strict** and improve the reliability of the data

Reliability

Context

We all believe that we control most aspects of our lives; the way we feel about ourselves (self-esteem) and even our physical state is affected by our feelings of control. People who lose that control often have physical and psychological consequences, such as depression and poorer recovery from illness.

Rotter (1966) introduced the idea of 'locus of control' (locus is Latin for 'place'). He was distinguishing between feeling you are in control (internal locus), and the feeling that events or other people are controlling you (external locus). Internal locus was seen as preferable for psychological health.

Lab studies have shown that having **control helps to reduce anxiety**. Stotland & Blumenthal (1964) told their participants that they would be sitting tests and then gave some the choice about the order in which they sat the tests. It was found that those who were allowed a choice showed less anxiety measured by sweatiness.

Langer et al. (1975) found that hospital patients who felt a greater sense of control requested fewer pain relievers and the nurses judged them to be less anxious.

Seligman (1975) linked lack of control to depression. He argued that people develop **'learned helplessness'** when they feel persistently unable to control their life. These permanent feelings lead to depression.

Ellen Langer had been working for some time in the area of **perceived control** (how in control you think you are). She had published *The Illusion of Control* (1975), about the psychological and health effects of believing that you are controlling your life, even if you largely are not. She thought this was a particular problem for the elderly into residential care.

'Illusion of control' is one of several heuristics or decision-making biases that human thinking exhibits.

Ferrare (1962) had found some startling evidence: he questioned a number of elderly people and found that 17 had no alternative but to move in to an old people's home. Out of those 17, eight had died within 4 weeks of moving in and a further eight had died after 10 weeks – the deaths were unexpected.

Judy Rodin was working in the same area of study, and she joined forces with Ellen Langer. They observed life in several nursing homes before approaching one home to set up their experiment. The director there had wanted to improve activities and control and was willing to allow an experiment that gave residents actual control of some aspects of their lives.

Aim

To compare a situation of **enhanced control** against the normal situation in a residential home, and to measure the consequences over a 24-month period, both in the quality of experience and in measurable outcomes such as mortality rates.

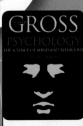

p.311

Critical assessment

Rodin & Langer (1977) followed up the residents with a further study, which showed that mortality rates in the responsibility-induced group (RIG) were half those in the comparison group (CG). However the CG rate was higher than the previous average for the home. This seemed to indicate a negative impact on CG, a result that was echoed by Shultz & Hanusa (1978). In a similar study, they showed that after the withdrawal of control at the end of a study, mortality rate in RIG dramatically increased. This shows the dramatic impact of loss of control on health, which many elderly people experience when first entering care homes. It also suggests extreme ethical caution when conducting life-altering field experiments and certainly highlights ethical issues with Langer & Rodin's study.

Langer *et al.* (1988) showed that elderly people who had experience of living with the elderly (grandparents) before the age of 13 acted out a 'younger' version of old age and were independently rated as more alert, active and independent than those who did not have the experience. This shows that we learn or are taught how to get old, and therefore can 'learn' to be 'younger'; there is a profound social effect on behaviour, a finding that supports Langer & Rodin.

Langer (1990) tested older adults (aged between 70 and 75) before and after a 5-day retreat where they spent the time living as though they were 20 years younger. A control group also participated in a retreat, but referred only to the past in discussions. Both groups showed improved intellectual functioning and health, but the active group showed greater improvements, which supports Langer & Rodin's study in that doing something active has the most effect.

Levy & Langer (1994) used a cross-cultural sample of hearing and deaf adults. The deaf adults were unlikely to have been exposed to routine stereotypes of ageing, and they showed better memory performance than the hearing adults. Chinese adults also outperformed American ones; Chinese culture has less negative stereotypes of the elderly, again showing the effect of social environment on health – supporting Langer & Rodin's findings.

Essentially, Langer and her colleagues showed that ageing is in fact as much a **cultural construct** (created and maintained as a norm in a culture) as an individual one, and that control and choice are key factors in the 'ageing' role-behaviours that individuals display, even down to memory test performance.

The effect on residential care of these findings has been mixed, but some local authorities in the UK have established 'group living' homes, where residents live communally in small groups within a residential home. This has been successful in improving all aspects of psychological health, as well as many physical indicators, including life expectancy.

As well as the studies listed in 'Critical assessment'. This question **can** be answered by **also** using:
- comparison with studies in the 'context'
- criticisms from 'evaluation of method'.

Use at least **four** clear points or comparisons in total.

Procedure

Sample:

- 91 residents aged 65–90 from two floors of the nursing home took part.
- Some residents were omitted from the research as they were bedridden, non-communicative or of a different age.
- The participants were assigned (dependent on which floor they lived on) to either the experimental or the control group.
- The experimental group was the responsibility-induced group (RIG), while the control group was the comparison group (CG).
- 39 women and 8 men were in RIG, and 35 women and 9 men were in CG.

Design:

The study took place in a nursing home in Connecticut, USA. 98 was a field experiment

The IV was the extent to which individuals were given responsibility and choice. The DV was 'well-being', as measured by questionnaires and behavioural measures.

Each group received a talk from the director of the home.

In the RIG talk, individual responsibility was emphasised. The participants were allowed to choose a plant to look after, have a choice over how their furniture was arranged and to pick Thursday or Friday as 'film night'.

In CG, the talk emphasised the staff's responsibility for the residents. Participants were given a plant and told that the staff would look after it, and were told what night was scheduled as 'film night'.

▲ **Figure 9.1**

Measurement:

- Two questionnaires were used.
- Each questionnaire was handed out a week before the briefing and then again after 3 weeks in order to assess the effects of the increased sense of personal control.
- The first questionnaire was completed by a research assistant, while the second was completed by two nurses.
- These were unaware of the research experimental hypothesis (double-blind design).
- The residents were also assessed on behavioural measures, such as going to film night, participation in competitions and the use of wheelchairs.

Findings

- Residents in RIG improved in all respects. They became more happy, active and alert, spending more time with others and feeling more 'in control'.

- Residents in CG decreased in all of these respects except control. The decreases are expected, but what is surprising is the increase in the sense of control in CG. The researchers chose to ignore this finding as many participants failed to understand the question (20 per cent).

- One final measure was a rating of overall function given by nursing staff at the beginning and the end of the research.
  - In CG, 71 per cent were judged to have worsened over the 3-week period.
  - In RIG, 93 per cent showed an overall improvement.

Variable (scale out of 8)	Change in control group	Change in experimental group
Control	+ 0.41	+ 1.6
Happiness	- 0.12	+ 0.28
Activity	- 1.28	+ 0.2
Alertness	- 0.37	+ 0.29
Visiting others (hours)	- 3.3	+ 6.78

▲ **Figure 9.2** A perceived lack of control can lead to depression

Conclusions

- Responsibility and choice are clearly **important determinants** of well-being in institutionalised older adults.
- Simply treating people 'kindly' – giving them plants, films and comfortably arranged rooms actually **reduces** happiness, alertness and activity.
- Offering individuals choice and responsibility, however, **increases** well-being in these respects.

Evaluation of methodology – strengths and weaknesses

Design

✔ Field experiment, so enhanced **ecological validity**
✔ **Random** assignment of conditions
✔ **Double-blind design** where measurement of variables was either objective or conducted by people who had no knowledge of the research hypothesis
✔ A **sound experimental design** and execution of study

✘ Control of variables is diminished in a field experiment

Sample

✔ Possibly **representative** of people in care homes for the elderly
✔ Reasonably **well-matched** experimental and control groups

✘ Not representative of elderly people in general, over 90 per cent of whom stay in their own homes for the whole of their life
✘ A small sample

Ethics

✔ No resident was treated **any worse** than they would have been normally.

✘ Problems of consent
✘ If the researchers believed that giving responsibility would improve health, they did not treat the control group fairly
✘ Issues relating to debrief – a full debrief may have led to relatives suing the home!
✘ Were the researchers 'playing God' with people's lives?

Validity

✔ Focus on realistic tasks and responsibilities, so **high mundane realism**

✔ The home was offering a very high level of care in general, so any differences were **very significant**

✘ No means of controlling nursing staff's conversations, so possible that some staff had guessed what was going on; this may have compromised validity

✘ Experimental group had higher initial sociability, so this may be a confounding variable — the two groups were not initially equal

▲ Figure 9.3

Reliability

✔ High degree of correlation between different nurses for measures of the same patient, so **inter-rater reliability** established

Context

Depth perception is made possible by having two components, **binocular** vision and **stereopsis**. Binocular vision is defined as vision where both eyes are aimed simultaneously at the same visual target and where both eyes work together as a coordinated team. Stereopsis is defined as vision where two separate images from two eyes are successfully combined into one image in the brain. So in order to perceive depth, the necessary brain developments to support these processes must take place.

There are many species of animal that emerge more or less fully developed at birth (**precocial** animals). Human babies, like most other mammals, are relatively helpless and require a long period of development. It is obvious that babies react to visual stimuli from birth, but what they can actually see is difficult to work out. It is certainly likely that abilities will be relatively modular or unconnected, and the effect of the environment will be to facilitate connections in the brain.

A long-standing argument in human development was the relative contribution of genes (**nature**) and interaction with the environment (**nurture**). Partly this was a religious argument about what was 'God-given', but for the Jesuits at least, what made a person was determined by their environment in early life. This argument had political importance, as things genetic were thought to be unchanging and therefore not worth trying to change socially.

A lot of research effort was directed towards discovering what was genetic and what developed later. However, very little research had been done on infant vision until after the Second World War, when a research centre for the psychological study of vision was established by Eleanor and Jack Gibson at Cornell University. The Gibsons' basic theory was that features of the environment determined much of visual development via innate mechanisms.

Lashley (1934) showed that rats could jump distance accurately even when reared in the dark. Eleanor Gibson thought this was a product of the training experience in teaching them to jump, so set out to observe depth perception; it was thought to be useful to contrast human children with precocial animals.

Aim

To use observational techniques to investigate depth perception in both human and animal infants, using a visual illusion of depth (called the 'visual cliff').

GROSS
PSYCHOLOGY

pp.250–1

Critical assessment

Walk & Hodge (1962) went on to show that a **monocular** (one-eyed) infant tested on the 'visual cliff' crawled over glass which had a patterned surface just beneath it and would not cross glass which had the same pattern 40 inches below its surface. Since this infant, using only monocular visual cues, was able to discriminate depth, the experiment suggests that binocular cues are not necessary for depth perception.

Infants who are several months old might have learnt about depth perception from experience. There is some intriguing evidence pointing to the importance of learning in the visual cliff situation. Nine-month-old infants had faster heart rates than normal when placed on the deep side, presumably because they were frightened (Campos et al. 1978). Research on the visual cliff therefore does not necessarily indicate that fear of depth is innate.

However, infants aged between 2 and 5 months actually had slower heart rates than usual when placed on the deep side, suggesting that they were not frightened. This slowing of heart rate probably reflected interest, and it certainly indicates that they detected some difference between the deep and shallow sides of the visual cliff situation – thus supporting Gibson & Walk.

Bower et al. (1970) obtained more convincing evidence that infants have some aspects of depth perception. They showed two objects to infants under 2 weeks old. One was large and approached to within 20 centimetres of the infant, whereas the other was small and approached to 8 centimetres. The two objects had the same retinal size (i.e. size at the retina) at their closest point to the infant. In spite of this, the infants were more disturbed by the object that came closer to them, rotating their heads upwards and pulling away from it. Apparently these infants somehow made use of information about depth to identify which object posed the greater threat. This suggests that some element of depth perception is innate, thus supporting Gibson & Walk.

Tracking studies look at the ability of children to follow a moving object. Tondel & Candy (2007) showed that even babies of 2 months old could track a moving clown figure, which supports Gibson & Walk's conclusion. However, other evidence suggests that it is the basic ability to detect large changes that is present at birth, but development of fine perceptual abilities requires time and learning.

In conclusion, research tends to show that some abilities are present close to birth, but some require experience to develop, and full depth perception is likely to follow this pattern. Gibson & Walk were both right and wrong!

▲ **Figure 9.4** Blue wildebeest calves are precocial: they can stand in minutes and run with the herd within hours. Human babies, on the other hand, are relatively helpless for a long time after birth

As well as the studies listed in 'Critical assessment'. This question **can** be answered by **also** using:
● comparison with studies in the 'context'
● criticisms from 'evaluation of method'.
Use at least **four** clear points or comparisons in total.

Procedure

The apparatus – the 'visual cliff'– was a glass tabletop, under which a drop in surface could be simulated using a patterned cloth. There was a 'shallow' side and a 'deep' side, separated by a narrow centre-board.

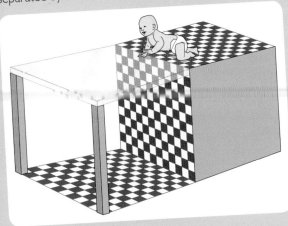

▲ **Figure 9.5**

Part 1:

- Sample of 36 human babies aged between 6 and 14 months (and their mothers!).
- A child was placed on the centre-board of the visual cliff apparatus.
- Their mother called to them from the deep side, then from the shallow side.
- Their movements were observed by two observers using standardised recording methods.

Part 2:

- A selection of young animals were tested (rats, puppies, kittens).
- A selection of precocial animals were tested – ones that could move within 24 hours of birth – chicks, goat kids, lambs and turtles.
- They were placed on the centre-board and their movements recorded.

Part 3:

- The kids and lambs were retested using a movable cliff surface.

Part 4:

- The cliff surface, which was patterned, was replaced by a uniform grey surface to detect the influence of pattern on depth perception.

Findings

Type	Age	Deep or shallow?	Other
Humans	6–14 months	27 moved to the shallow side 3 moved to the deep side 6 stayed on the centreboard	Most showed distress at any sight of deep side
Chickens	24 hours or less	Total refusal to move to deep side	
Turtles		76% shallow side 24% deep	Expected to use deep side as aquatic species with no fear of depth
Rats	Infants Adults	Shallow side always No preference for either side	Adults use touch from whiskers rather than vision, so can feel glass
Lambs	3 days or less	Total refusal to move near to the deep side	
Goals	3 days or less	Total refusal to move near to the deep side	
Kittens	4 weeks	Total refusal to move near to the deep side	

- The infants who moved to the deep side may have had developmental motor control problems as this movement was backing onto or resting on the deep side.
- In Part 3 the animals reacted by 'freezing' when the surface was dropped more than 30cm; the animal did not adapt or habituate when the process was repeated several times.
- In Part 4, with the uniform grey surface, the animals did not prefer either the deep or the shallow side.

Conclusions

- Major aspects of depth perception are present in infants, and are possibly present at birth, but **some aspects are learnt**.
- Depth perception appears to be **innate in some species**.
- Depth perception involves **interpreting changes in pattern that indicate depth**.

◀ **Figure 9.6** A selection of young animals were tested including kids

Evaluation of methodology – strengths and weaknesses

Design

✔ **Controlled observation** under laboratory conditions
✔ Apparatus allowed the use of senses other than vision to be eliminated

✗ Method needs mobile animals; human crawlers and toddlers have time to learn depth perception in the previous 6 months

Sampling

✗ Humans are qualitatively different as they are not precocial animals — that is, they require a long nurturing period and are not ready for survival soon after birth
✗ Sample size was small and the age range was very large

Ethics

✗ The humans, as well as some animal participants, demonstrated considerable distress during the procedure
✗ Use of non-human animals in research is acceptable if alleviating human suffering, but not just for 'intellectual curiosity' (Dawkins 1990), which calls the methodology into question

✔ Method is easily **replicable** and **reliable**, producing reliable results

Reliability

◀ **Figure 9.7** Some children and animals experienced distress during the experiment

✘ Validity has been compromised when studies using younger humans with more sophisticated methods showed that elements of depth perception were present

Validity

✔ The presence of encouraging mothers in the procedure meant that the toddlers' refusal was more convincing and therefore results were more **valid**

Context

Evolutionary psychology assumes that some important behaviours are 'genetically prepared'. This means that the behaviours have been selected under environmental pressures over thousands and even millions of years for their survival value. Modern behaviour and the influence of culture are seen as a surface appearance that is in reality largely driven by genes.

Evolutionary psychologists believe that our important behaviours were selected for in an Environment of Evolutionary Adaptation (EEA), which is assumed to be east African grasslands and forest margins (savannah), and that this was a period of more than a million years.

The slight difference in size between male and female humans suggests that our species is slightly promiscuous (small number of partners) rather than monogamous. In similarly sized species males tend to focus on the fertility and availability of the female, whereas females tend to favour males who show some survival characteristics, such as strength, size and ability, to find resources (likely to be found in mature males).

Sexual selection (mating) in humans is presumed to show sex differences in strategy:

1. **Parental investment** (Trivers 1972) means that females will choose males with good resources, to protect and ensure the welfare of offspring.
2. **Paternal probability** (Daly et al. 1982) means that males will seek females who will bear their children and no one else's (e.g. virgins).
3. **Reproductive value** (Symons 1979) suggests that males will seek signs of fertility in females (young, healthy-looking, high energy levels, wide hips).

Thus evolutionary predictions for humans would be that females would look for wealth and material possessions (likely to be found in older males) and males for youth and good looks in females (signs of reproductive health).

It is difficult to draw conclusions from our nearest cousins, the primates, as they have evolved separately for over 6 million years. Equally, all humans apart from us have become extinct. The only way to investigate would be cross-cultural comparisons – if behaviours are the same worldwide, it would suggest a possible genetic control of mating. If different, then mating would differ from one culture to another and would not be genetically controlled.

Aim

Buss intended to test evolutionary theories of mate selection by asking a large, cross-cultural sample for the factors most important in selection of a mate.

▲ **Figure 10.1** False stereotype or theory?

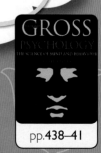

GROSS
PSYCHOLOGY
THE SCIENCE OF MIND AND BEHAVIOUR

pp.438–41

Critical assessment

- Not all Buss's claims are fully supported by his own data (e.g. paternal probability).
- Focus on heterosexual mating alone.

However, there is substantial evidence to show that mate preference in heterosexuals is influenced by considerations of fertility:

- Singh (1993) showed that a waist–hip ratio (WHR) in women of 0.7 has been considered most attractive for the last 50 years in Western media. This WHR shows wider hips that indicate fertility.
- Singh believes it acts as a filter, after which face and/or body weight are used in most cultures (Swami & Furnham 2006).
- Most people across cultures prefer those with symmetrical faces and bodies; it is likely that physical symmetry equates with reproductive fitness (Cartwright 2000; Little 2007))
- Men rate women as more attractive when they are ovulating (Roberts et al. 2004), despite female human ovulation being barely detectable.
- Female sexual desire tends to be highest at or just before ovulation (Pillsworth et al. 2004).
- Schmitt (2003) conducted an even larger cross-cultural study (16,288 participants in 53 countries) and found similar results to Buss.

The following should also be considered:

- Human mating tends to reflect cultural history, which is an interaction between economic status, economic history, religious history, penetration of global culture into older traditions and so on – hence the variation and exceptions in many studies.
- Global culture (e.g. Coca-Cola and McDonalds), as spread by mass media, obscures cultural differences; it emphasises male political dominance (patriarchy) and resources as desirable for mating. Mass movements like patriarchal religions tend to do likewise. Data are biased by social forces.
- Equally, human tribes may well have evolved cultural practices in mating from an original practice 70,000 years old (when the human population was probably fewer than 10,000 individuals), which emphasised movement of unattached fertile females from clan to clan – requiring no biological explanation.

The biggest criticism of the evolutionary psychology viewpoint comes from the people providing the scientific evidence – palaeo-anthropologists, geneticists and so on (Stringer 2010; Jones 2009; Rose & Rose 2000):

- There is no existing physical evidence of mating behaviour in prehistory (before writing), so hypotheses cannot have material support.
- The idea of the EEA is largely discredited, as human evolution is an immensely complex puzzle that played out over several million years and many, rapidly changing, environments.
- Since the size of human groups until recently was very small, lifespans were typically less than 30 years and human contact between groups probably minimal (hunter-gatherers do not stay in one place), so it is unlikely that mating involved weighing up any of Buss's factors – rather it was a matter of necessity with whoever was available!
- The whole area of research is contaminated by modern stereotypes of the past rather than informed by scientific evidence.

Procedure

Sample:

- 37 samples from 33 countries on six continents.
- 10,047 participants.
- 5,446 female, 4,601 male.
- Sample sizes from 1,491 (USA) to 55 (Iran).
- Age range 17–28.
- Mean age 23.

Sampling technique:

- Varied between countries – for example, Germany: through newspaper ~~advert; Venezuela: systemic sample of every fifth house in a group of~~ neighbourhoods of differing socio-economic class; South Africa: rural Zulu sample required questions read to them.

Researchers:

- Mostly native residents.
- Unaware of research hypotheses.
- Three bilingual translators collaborated on each research area.
- All questions had to be gender-neutral in the native language (so no research bias could be detected by respondents).
- Questionnaires were modified to be culturally relevant (e.g. polygamous societies as in Nigerian sample).

Questionnaires:

1. Rating of 18 variables on a 4-point scale (0–3) including four target variables (virginity, chastity, looks, financial prospects) + biographical data + wishes relating to marriage, children and so on.
2. Ranking 13 characteristics in order of importance including two target characteristics (physical attractiveness and financial status).

> As well as the studies listed in 'Critical assessment'.
> This question **can** be answered by **also** using:
> - comparison with studies in the 'context'
> - criticisms from 'evaluation of method'.
> Use at least **four** clear points or comparisons in total.

◄ **Figure 10.2** Physical attractiveness was one of the variables that were asked about in the study

Findings

Age:
- In all 37 cultures woman's ideal man was older than themselves.
- In all 37 cultures man's ideal woman was younger than themselves.
- Average age difference was 4 years.

Ideal mate age:
- Ideal woman: 24.83
- Ideal man: 28.81

Ambition and finance:
- In 36 out of 37 cultures women placed significantly more emphasis on male financial prospects than males did for females.
- Only in Spain was this reversed.
- Women ruled ambition and industriousness in men more than men did for women in 29 cultures.
- In three cultures the pattern was reversed, with women being highly rated for ambition and industriousness.

Good looks:
- In all 37 cultures, men rated good looks as being more important than women did.

Chastity (lack of sexual experience):
- Highly variable response that generally linked to religiosity in a culture.
- Ireland was the only country in Western Europe that rated this factor highly.
- Men placed more emphasis on chastity than women did in general in all cultures.

▲ Figure 10.3

Conclusions

- Females valued **resources** as indicated by the high ratings for male financial prospects, ambition and industriousness.
- This supports the **parental investment** hypothesis.
- Males valued youth and physical **attractiveness** more highly than women, these being indicators of fertility.
- This supports the **reproductive value** hypothesis.
- Males valued **chastity** more than females, though this was not a universal finding. Buss, however, takes this as support for the paternal probability hypothesis.

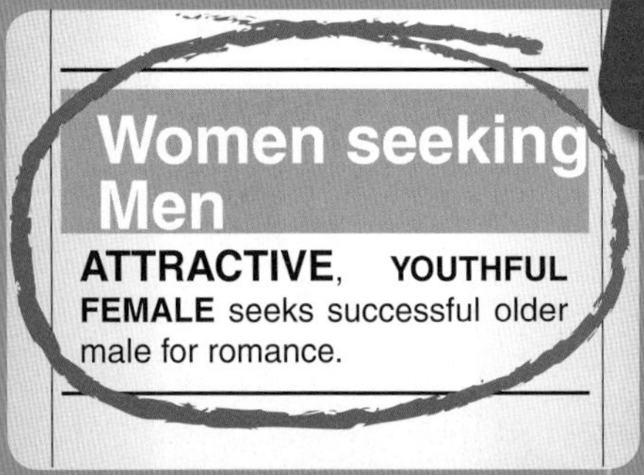

Women seeking Men
ATTRACTIVE, **YOUTHFUL FEMALE** seeks successful older male for romance.

▲ **Figure 10.4** Females valued resources and males valued youth and attractiveness

Evaluation of methodology – strengths and weaknesses

Design

✔ A **large** cross-sectional and cross-cultural study that was very ambitious in its scope

✗ Self-report studies such as questionnaires are always open to various types of bias (e.g. lying, conforming to social norms)

Sample

✔ A **very large** overall sample size, which increases the generalisability of findings

✗ Sample sizes **varied greatly** and were in some cases very small (e.g. Iran with 55 respondents)

✗ Overrepresented by Western participants from industrialised nations (77%)

✗ Samples in many cases were **not representative** of the parent populations

✗ Sampling techniques varied greatly, showing **low internal reliability**

Ethics

✔ Questionnaires were modified to **avoid offence** in differing cultures

✔ Two separate measures used, which reduces chances of **extraneous variables** affecting ratings

✔ Questionnaires modified to provide as **identical meanings** as possible in differing cultures

Validity

✘ Self-report biases make it possible that data were seriously distorted either through **fear of non-conformity**, being discovered (very real in some societies) or making oneself look good!

✘ Participant bias may include **guessing** the research purpose from the questionnaire

◀ **Figure 10.5** This is a large cross-cultural study, but there was still an overrepresentation of Western participants

Reliability

✘ Low internal reliability due to differing sampling techniques

Context

At the time when Rosenhan was carrying out this study, doctors specialising in mental disorders had been the people who decided whether someone had a mental disorder for over a century. Known as 'alienists' until the early twentieth century, psychiatrists remain to this day the legal 'gatekeepers' of treatment of mental disorder.

Systems to help the psychiatrists were developed in Europe and the USA, which are now large diagnostic manuals (ICD and DSM) – essentially the rules for diagnosis. Nevertheless, there is a lot of leeway in judging someone's mental state, and then further leeway in treating a disorder.

Questions had been asked about the **validity** and **reliability** of psychiatric diagnosis with increasing frequency after the Second World War. In 1956, Bateson drew attention to the social relationships of schizophrenics, arguing that family behaviour was a major factor in the onset and maintenance of the illness. The validity issue was whether someone was correctly diagnosed; the reliability issue was whether different psychiatrists come up with the same diagnosis.

A developing movement in Europe and the USA – often called the 'antipsychiatry movement' – formed around R.D. Laing in the 1960s. Laing had trained at the Tavistock Institute in London and started an influential community project in London, where the disordered and their carers lived together in a large mansion. Laing questioned the nature of mental illness – though not its reality – and also questioned the medical bias to diagnosis and treatment. While his approach was initially influential and continued into the 1980s, it made little impact on the treatment of disorders. A final factor was the emergence of evidence from Russia in the late 1960s that psychiatric diagnosis was used as an instrument of political control. Therefore the cultural climate of the time was highly critical of psychiatric diagnosis.

Rosenhan was studying the legal aspects of mental disorder, where it is crucial to establish whether an offender is mentally disordered or not, especially for the trial. Medical professionals are often asked for expert opinion about someone's mental state. 'Sane' and 'insane' are legal terms relating to the criminal justice process, not medical ones, and relate to the person's understanding of the world about them.

Aim

The aim of the study was to critically investigate the diagnosis of mental illness and whether mental health professionals could actually tell the difference between people who had disorders and people who did not.

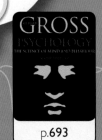

GROSS PSYCHOLOGY
THE SCIENCE OF MIND AND BEHAVIOUR

p.693

Critical assessment

This study had very serious implications for psychiatric diagnosis at the time, suggesting a lack of validity in diagnosis and also a lack of inter-rater reliability between members of the medical staff.

Falke & Moser (1975) found that agreement between doctors on diagnoses of angina, emphysema and tonsillitis (without lab tests) were no better than for schizophrenia, lending support to Rosenhan's hypothesis.

Rosenhan's study received considerable criticism, especially by Spitzer (1976). Most criticism centred around Rosenhan's selective reportage of experiences, and incredulity that psychiatrists could misdiagnose so consistently. However, the major criticism of this study came from Wolitsky (1975), who pointed out that psychiatrists err on the side of caution for a multitude of reasons, and should be expected to admit the pseudopatients just to be on the safe side (false positive bias). This suggested that Rosenhan's findings lacked validity.

Diagnosis itself has improved radically since the experiments, including dropping homosexuality as a disorder in the 1980s. There are, however, a number of significant differences between DSM and the European ICD system, which lessen the validity of the results for Europe. When this study took place, the DSM used was the second version – now it is in the fourth edition, which itself has been revised. Many of the criteria for judging mental disorder have been tightened up, so it suggests that Rosenhan's conclusions are dated and lacking validity.

One of Rosenhan's pseudopatients had his (largely positive) stay in hospital unreported, which suggests selective reporting. However, this pseudopatient also confirms that he *was* diagnosed as a schizophrenic, as were the others.

Slater (2004), a clinical psychologist and author, allegedly repeated Rosenhan's method, and claimed to receive medication and diagnosis in response to fake symptoms. Spitzer *et al.* (2005) powerfully criticised Slater, and ran their own study, where 76 psychiatrists – in response to a brief case study – largely contradicted Slater's claims, and suggested that studies like Rosenhan's were less likely to succeed today. Other inaccuracies in Slater's book cast further doubt on her claims (Moran 2006). This lowers the level of support for Rosenhan's hypothesis.

Rosenhan's study is certainly scientifically questionable, but may have helped to tighten up diagnosis in the USA at the time. It has also highlighted that diagnosis is not a simple dichotomy between 'sick' and 'well', but involves making a decision on a continuum of human behaviour between 'normal' and 'abnormal' (Pilgrim 2000).

As well as the studies listed in 'Critical assessment'. This question **can** be answered by **also** using:
- comparison with studies in the 'context'
- criticisms from 'evaluation of method'.

Use at least **four** clear points or comparisons in total.

Procedure

Experiment 1

Design: Participant observation.

Participants:

- Eight confederates (friends and colleagues of Rosenhan).
- (Five men, three women).
- Called 'pseudopatients'.
- The real participants were hospital staff who did not know about the experiment.

Settings: Twelve psychiatric hospitals. Some pseudopatients stayed in more than one hospital (so 12 diagnoses in total).

Procedure:

- Pseudopatient called hospital for an appointment, complaining of having heard voices saying 'empty', 'hollow' and 'thud' (auditory hallucinations).
- Pseudopatients gave false names, occupations and symptoms, but gave real life histories.
- Once on ward, pseudopatients stopped pretending symptoms, behaved normally and wrote observations.
- Pseudopatients could only be discharged when they convinced staff that they were in remission.
- Hospital records examined after completion of study.

▲ **Figure 10.6**

Experiment 2

Design: Observation.

Setting: Research and teaching hospital where staff were aware of original study's findings.

Participants: Hospital staff.

Procedure:

- Staff told that one or more pseudopatients would attempt to be admitted in the next 3 months.
- For every new patient, each staff member rated the likelihood that they were an impostor.
- There were no pseudopatients; all attending admissions were real patients not involved in the study.

Findings

Experiment 1

Quantitative:

- All patients gained admission.
- Diagnosed as schizophrenic (one as manic depressive).
- Range of stay between 7 and 52 days (average 19).

Qualitative:

- Discharges given as 'schizophrenia in remission' (remission means 'gone away').
- No pseudopatient challenged by a doctor, but often challenged by fellow patients (35/118 recorded individual patient interactions).

Normal behaviour was pathologised (e.g. 'abnormal' writing behaviour, waiting for lunch outside dining room was 'oral fixation'). Normal medical staff interactions were minimal. Pseudopatients felt powerless and depersonalised. Pseudopatients did not take medication, and neither did many real patients!

Experiment 2

Quantitative:

- 193 patients admitted.
- 41 alleged to be impostors by members of staff.
- 23 suspected by one psychiatrist.
- 19 suspected by a psychiatrist and a staff member jointly.
- All were genuine patients.

Conclusions

- Psychiatrists tend to a **'false positive' diagnosis** (known in science as a 'Type 2 error').
- Normal (sane) behaviour **not easily detected** in mental hospitals ('insane places').
- Behaviour is interpreted according to the **expectations of the medical staff**.
- Once diagnosed, patients are **expected** to be disordered.
- Rosenhan called this 'the **stickiness of diagnostic labels**'.
- Medical staff, including psychiatrists, **cannot tell the difference** between mentally disordered and normal behaviour.

▲ **Figure 10.7** Normal behaviour such as note-taking was pathologised

Evaluation of the methodology – strengths and weaknesses

Design

✔ **High ecological validity**
✔ No one knew they were being observed, so **natural behaviour in general**
✔ **No demand characteristics**
✔ Diagnosis data and staff comments **confirmed from records**

✘ Difficult to record some behaviour objectively
✘ Very difficult to replicate

Sample

✔ The 12 hospitals in the first experiment were a **representative cross-section** of public and private facilities, staff ratios, age of facility and so on

✘ Still a relatively small sample, and in the second experiment, merely one hospital

Ethics

✔ All data were kept confidential

✘ Strong degree of deception used
✘ No consent by participants (medical staff)
✘ Pseudopatients took up the time of medical staff that could have been given to genuine patients
✘ Unlikely that any debrief information left staff feeling as they were before the event, and probably made them angry and lowered self-esteem
✘ Were genuine patients harmed, especially as a result of the second observation?

Validity

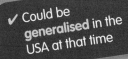

✔ Could be **generalised** in the USA at that time

✗ Culture-specific in terms of place and time; practices different in other cultures, and many changes have occurred over the 40 years since the original studies

▲ **Figure 10.8** The medical staff were the participants in this experiment

✗ Because of the mixed nature of replication results, **external validity** may not be very high

Reliability

✔ The procedure had high **internal reliability** as all pseudopatients had similar experiences

DOING THE METHODS QUESTION

The question: A) Outline one advantage and one disadvantage of using [a method] in this research (3)

- **One** advantage and **one** disadvantage for each of the common methods.
- **THINK – LINK** for **either** the advantage **or** the disadvantage **or both**.

Method	Advantage	Disadvantage
Observation	• Real-life behaviour in its natural environment	• No control over any variables • Observer may be biased in recording data
Experiment (lab)	• Higher degree of control over variables	• May be a very artificial environment (lacks realism) • Lacks total control over all variables
Experiment (field)	• (Fairly) real-life behaviour in its natural environment	
Experiment (natural)	• Independent variable (IV) occurs naturally in the real world	• No control over the IV
Correlation	• Shows relationship between variables	• Cannot show cause–effect relationships between variables
Case study	• Lots of detailed qualitative information	• Cannot generalise to other cases or the population

The question: B) Identify one issue of reliability in this research and describe how you would deal with this issue of reliability (3)

- A definition of reliability related to the scenario.
- **THINK – LINK** using **one** of the two methods below.
- One way of ensuring reliability in research.
  1. Repeat the research using the same method and the same sample.
  2. Repeat the research using the same method and a different sample.

The question: C) Identify one issue of validity in this research and describe how you would deal with this issue of validity (3)

- A definition of validity related to the scenario.
- **THINK – LINK** using **one** of the three methods below.
  3. Ensure that the dependent variable (DV) is actually measuring what it is supposed to be measuring.
  4. Ensure that your variables are related to the problem you are investigating (*construct validity*).
  5. Check your method and result against a well-established method or well-established set of results (*concurrent validity*).

The question: D) Outline one advantage and one disadvantage [of a sampling method] in this research (3)

- **One** advantage and **one** disadvantage for **each** of the common methods of sampling.
- **THINK – LINK** in **either** advantage **or** disadvantage **or both**.

Sampling method	Advantage	Disadvantage
Opportunity	• Easy to arrange and select participants	• Not representative of the population • May be biased by the experimenter towards their hypothesis
Self-selecting (volunteer)	• No problems of consent	• Volunteers tend to be different from non-volunteers and not representative of population • Initially very time-consuming
Random	• The most scientific method	• People may refuse to take part • Difficult to organise
Systematic	• A scientific method	• People may refuse to take part • Difficult to organise
Stratified	• Has correct proportions from the population (e.g. male and female)	• Time-consuming to gain a sample • People may refuse to take part

Overview

- Six questions are set.
- They occur in the same order.
- The only things that change are the words in the square brackets […].

All answers must contain a key phrase or sentence that quotes part of the scenario or uses material from the scenario.

THINK – LINK

The question: F) State one conclusion that can be drawn from [some feature of the results table] in this research (3)

- You must **state the obvious** from the table or chart.
- You must **include every detail**, not just a conclusion.
- Remember that three marks means 3 minutes of writing time – there should be at least two long sentences:
  1. Literal description of the data display.
  2. Conclusion to be drawn from the data display.

Mean recall of words in memory test

Trained condition	Control condition
13.4	8.8

- **Bad:** Memory was better in the trained than the control condition.
- **Good:** The mean recall in the trained condition (13.4) was substantially higher than the mean recall in the control condition (8.8). This suggests that the training regime led to improved recall in this experiment.

The question: E) Discuss one ethical issue that might arise in this research (3)

- Definition of a common ethical issue using the words of the scenario.
- THINK – LINK saying how the issue might arise.
- Use one of the four most common uses:
  - Lack of informed consent (say how it might arise in this scenario).
  - Deception (say how it might arise in this scenario).
  - Failure to protect participants physically or psychologically (say how it might arise in this scenario).
  - Inadequate debriefing (say how it might arise in this scenario).

I like to answer questions in the order they are set

- Do what you feel is most comfortable.
- You must be extra strict about time limits; you actually have a maximum of about 14 minutes per question, but play it safe!
- 4 minutes for Q1a.
- 8 minutes for Q1b. This is one of the questions where you can easily overrun.
- Leave spaces at the end of questions for additions if you have time to go back.
- 12 minutes for every 12-mark question.
- Be very careful about Q2. This is another question where you can easily overrun.
- Finish the paper (or lose grades!).

▲ Figure 12.1

A couple of days to go and I don't know enough!

- Prioritise your questions beforehand.
- Do the ones you know about first.
- Be strict about time limits, but make sure you write as much as you can for the ones you know well.
- If you know Q3 Strengths and Weaknesses, answer that one first.
- Start a new page for each question.
- Go back and add on material as you remember it.
- Add material to previous answers when you run out of questions you can do.
- Do not stop trying to remember material.
- Use the whole time in the exam.
- Do not give up!

I want to maximise my marks quickly

- Prioritise your questions beforehand.
- Q3 Strengths and Weaknesses is usually easy to remember and is worth as much as the other questions – so do that one first.
- Do the question you are strongest at next.
- Be careful about time limits.
- This is critical with Q1b, where many people overrun.
- Leave spaces at the end of questions for additions if you have time to go back.
- Use the time you make on the early questions to make some answers longer (e.g. Q2 Therapies).
- You can do the questions in any order you choose.
- Finish the paper (or lose grades!).

PY2 – WHICH STRATEGY SUITS YOU?

I like to answer questions in the order they are set

- Do what you feel is most comfortable.
- Do not spend more than 40 minutes on Section A.
- Leave spaces at the end of questions for additions if you have time to go back.
- Have a minimum of 20 minutes earmarked for Section C.
- If you are short of time, stop what you are doing, leave space and move on to doing Section C on a fresh page.
- Do your favourite Section B question first, but stick to the time limit of about 12 minutes.
- Finish the paper (or lose grades!).

A couple of days to go and I don't know enough!

- Prioritise your questions beforehand.
- Do the ones you know about first.
- You will probably remember Q2 Procedures and Q3 Findings and Conclusions; try to do these with a point-by-point approach (just leave out the bullets).
- Do not forget to label both Findings and Conclusions.
- Context and Aims are usually well remembered.
- Do not forget to label both Context and Aims.
- If you 'THINK – LINK' in Section 3, you cannot go wrong.
- Make sure you refer to the scenario in every answer.
- Leave space in every answer to come back and add material you may remember.

I want to maximise my marks quickly

- Prioritise your questions beforehand.
- Section C can be a quick way to gain marks – if you know your stuff, that is!
- Make sure you refer to the scenario in every answer you give.
- Section B has 20 chunks you need to know, so you are more likely to remember three of those.
- Section A has 30 chunks you need to know, however, you may be comfortable with Q2 Procedures first.
- You can do the questions in any order you choose.
- Finish the paper (or lose grades!).